The Eyes of Chief Seattle

*The Eyes of
Chief Seattle*

The Suquamish Museum

Acknowledgments

The catalogue for the exhibition *The Eyes of Chief Seattle* was funded in part by the National Endowment for the Humanities, with support from the Administration for Native Americans and the Norman Archibald Charitable Foundation.

Research for *The Eyes of Chief Seattle* was conducted by the staff of the Suquamish Tribal Cultural Center and Rod Slemmons. Information for the exhibition text and catalogue was taken from the writings of Erna Gunther, Myron Eells, T. T. Waterman, Barbara Lane, Jay Miller, Cindy Clark, Hillary Stewart, Warren Snyder, Nile Thompson, Carolyn Marr, Marian Smith, Pamela Amoss, J.E. Michael Kew, and Paula Gustafson.

Artifacts appear courtesy of the Thomas Burke Memorial Washington State Museum, Seattle's Museum of History and Industry, the Kitsap County Historical Society, the Bainbridge Island Historical Society, and the Suquamish Museum and its many friends.

Photographs from the Suquamish Tribal Archives were collected from members and friends of the Suquamish tribal community, the Historical Photography Collection of the University of Washington, the Burke Museum, the Museum of History and Industry, the Washington State Historical Society, the Kitsap County Historical Society, the Bancroft Library, the National Archives, the National Anthropological Archives/Smithsonian Institution, and the Whatcom Museum of History and Art.

We would like to give special thanks to Dr. Barbara Lane and Bill Holm for serving as consultants on the catalogue, to Bernard Adams for his community organization efforts, and to Richard Linzer for his invaluable contributions to the development of the museum.

Suquamish Tribal Cultural Center and Museum Staff: Carey Caldwell, Director; Charles Sigo, Tribal Curator; Susan Blalock, Research Director; Barbara Lawrence, Candi Bohlman, Marilyn Jones, and Leonard Forsman, Research and Museum Assistants; Leota Anthony, Vista Volunteer.

© 1985 by The Suquamish Museum. All rights reserved. No part of the contents of this book may be reproduced without the written permission of The Suquamish Museum. Published by The Suquamish Museum.

Cover: Puget Sound baskets
Back Cover: Interior of the Suquamish Museum
Frontispiece: Little Joe and wife (Snohomish) next to a large dugout canoe on the Tulalip Reservation

Catalogue Production and Photography: Rod Slemmons, Argentum Photographic Services, Seattle
Design and Production: Ed Marquand, Seattle
Typesetting: The Type Gallery, Seattle

Printed and bound in Japan by Nissha Printing Co., Ltd., Kyoto.

Library of Congress Catalog Card Number: 85–61395

Table of Contents

Preface 7
Introduction 9
Map 12
The Indians of Puget Sound 13
Winter Dwellings and Lifestyle 14
Suquamish Villages 16
Food Gathering and Preparation 18
Fishing 20
Basket Making 22
Matting 24
Weaving 26
Canoes 28
Spiritual Life 30
Tribal Alliances and Trade 33
The Treaties and Their Aftermath 34
Chief Seattle's Speech 36
The Advent of Reservation Life 38
Indian Boarding Schools 40
Changes in Land Ownership 42
Transition in Labor and Economy 44
Indians in the Military 46
Sports 48
The Suquamish Tribe Today 50
Exhibition Artifacts 52
Catalogue Photographs 55
Bibliography 56

Preface

In June 1983 a long-standing dream became a reality when the Suquamish Museum opened with its premier exhibition *The Eyes of Chief Seattle*. Over the previous six years the Suquamish Tribal Cultural Center documented Suquamish and Puget Sound Indian heritage by establishing an archive of historical photographs, oral histories, and written records. These materials create a foundation for new interpretations of American Indian history. Research focused on the last 130 years, the period of dramatic cultural transition beginning with the signing of the treaties with the United States government in the 1850s. The cultural center has since received national recognition for its study of Native American peoples and their struggle to adapt to the ways of a foreign culture.

Using resources gathered by the cultural center, the original *Eyes of Chief Seattle* exhibition was developed in collaboration with Rod Slemmons, then curator of the Museum of History and Industry in Seattle. The exhibition was presented at that museum in 1982, and subsequently traveled to Nantes, France, as a part of the Nantes/Seattle Sister City Program. Upon its return to the Suquamish Museum, it was greatly expanded with artifacts from the community and other museums in the Puget Sound area.

The cultural center's award-winning media production *Come Forth Laughing: Voices of the Suquamish People* added a new dimension to the exhibition in June 1984. It complements *The Eyes of Chief Seattle* by bringing to life the voices of the elders who are quoted extensively in the exhibit.

The research and collecting efforts of the Suquamish Tribal Cultural Center continue, aided by the establishment of the museum and ongoing educational and interpretive programs. *The Eyes of Chief Seattle* marks the beginning of an increased understanding, by the general public, of the lives and experiences of the original inhabitants of northwest Washington.

We would like to express our deepest thanks to the numerous individuals and institutions who have contributed to this effort. In particular, we are tremendously grateful to the elders of the Suquamish and other Puget Sound tribes who have generously shared their wisdom and knowledge with us. Their continued support has made our work possible and the message of survival in *The Eyes of Chief Seattle* an inspiration to people throughout the world.

Introduction

Lawrence Webster is a retired logger, like thousands of other men in northwest Washington. However, Webb, as he is known, is a member of a small and special group. He is an elder of the Suquamish Tribe and a speaker of the Puget Sound Salish language. The elders are bridges between two very different cultures and they have all adapted in their own way, at their own pace, preserving more or less of their own "Indianess." Much of what you read about in this catalogue was experienced firsthand by Webb and the other elders, and is still crisp in his legendary memory. Webb's wit, eloquence, and survivor's brand of hope were central to the efforts that resulted in the Suquamish Museum and The Eyes of Chief Seattle. *Born in 1899, Webb is a former Tribal Chairman and lives in Indianola, near where he was raised. The following is taken from an informal interview with him on the Port Madison Indian Reservation on February 2, 1985.*

The best childhood memories I can think of was when we used to gather down on the beach in front of the village where Chief Seattle Park is today. Children'd come down there...two...three, a couple of parents, and by late afternoon, I'd say maybe fifty percent of the tribe would be there either cooking or clam digging or just playing and swimming. That's where all the fun was in my childhood. I was going onto seven years old when the village broke up in 1906 and we all left. That was when the military bought the land there and the people got separated around the reservation.

The old people at that time called white people *pastəds* [pah-steds]. There wasn't much feeling that I can remember that we were different or discriminated against because the only white person around was the Indian Subagent, Bartow, who had a boy that I played with quite a bit. The time I first really noticed a difference in people was when we'd go to the store, in Poulsbo or Seattle. Then I couldn't figure out where all those *pastəds* came from!

I first went to the Indian boarding school in Tulalip in 1908, when I was in second grade, and stayed for four years. I got tired of it and wouldn't go back, so I went to the regular school at South Kingston. They let me stay for a year until they wouldn't let me back because we didn't pay property taxes. They kicked me out of the Miller Bay School for the same reason. After that I went to the Cushman Trade School. I finished grade school there and got a year and a half of high school at Lincoln Park. Then they wouldn't let us go there, so I just quit school and went to work. I worked for about fifty years after that.

When I was small, I heard very little English. About the only time you heard any English spoken was when old Bartow, the Subagent, would come and give a speech or ask questions. The Indians would give him his answers in English, but as soon as he left everybody was talking Indian again. One thing that hurt about the Indian boarding schools was that they wouldn't let you talk Indian. If they heard you, you were punished. A lot of the kids could hardly talk English when they got there. Kids got punished for other things, too...like not being right on time. It was more military than anything else. Another hard thing was that you didn't see your family. It took two days to get to Tulalip and there was no place for the families to stay. The kids were allowed to go home for Christmas, but they had to be back the next day, which made it impossible for those that didn't live right in Tulalip.

A few people in my generation had no interest in preserving the language or remembering the old ways. They probably thought that it wouldn't ever do them any good. They were too busy surviving. Lately, there has been more interest and the museum has gotten people interested in their history. The way

I've always felt about it, if you haven't got any memories of what your culture was back there, you just wonder what you're doing around here now.

The Suquamish always claimed they were better fishermen than the other Indians on Puget Sound, because they used to go fishing clear to Point Roberts in the early days. They lost a few men going up there in bad weather, from what I understand. Around here they would make weirs in small streams to get fish. They sometimes made them out of cedar nets or cattail mats used like a bag. They'd get them all running around in there and pull one end up and have a whole bag full of salmon. I've seen them do that a lot of times. But the favorite one, if the fish weren't running too heavy, was to put a weir across made out of cedar sticks and limbs. The fish would get their heads stuck in it and couldn't back out.

The men would bring the salmon over, the women would start cleaning them, and us kids would have to help. And you'd see two, three hundred salmon up smoking in one smokehouse. They used to smoke it so it was hard and dry, and toss it up in the attic and stack it for the winter. And another thing they started doing when I was a youngster was salting the fish down in barrels with rock salt. They also used to get clams and hunt deer and get seals from the bay.

In order to get cash, they would do some logging, close to the beaches, and sell the logs to the Port Madison and Port Gamble mills. They would also sell clams and fish at markets in Seattle. When I was very young, four or five, they would still take smoked salmon over to Seattle or Lake Washington and trade it with the people from up around Yakima or Snoqualmie. They'd trade back and forth. They used to paddle across Elliott Bay in the big canoes and camp there a short way south of what is now known as Yesler Way. That was mostly mud flats down there, but there were a few pieces of high ground, and that's where the Indians used to camp. Those big canoes were really seaworthy, even more so if they were loaded down. If it got rough, you could put up a small sail if you were going in the right direction. If you weren't, you just found a place to pull in and camp until the blow was over.

During the late 'teens and early 1920s when I first started logging it was mostly steam and railroad. Of course there was still some "skid road" logging around. I first started north of Seattle, near what they call Alderwood Manor now. Puget Mill was logging that off. They didn't have a bunkhouse out there, so I lived right in Seattle. I took the streetcar to the end of the line in the morning and then got on the company speeder and went to camp. Very few Indians from this part of the country got into steam logging right away, but as the business developed and high-lead logging came in, more and more Indians were on the crews.

Around 1919, a friend and I decided to get out of town and rode the freight trains as far east as Chicago and south to Texas. We stopped and worked at all kinds of odd jobs along the way, just bumming around. I longshored that winter when I got back, and one day I was sitting in the International Longshoremen Association Hall at the foot of Union street, waiting for a job when my dad, who I hadn't seen for years, shows up looking for me. He asked me to go fishing, trolling, with him on the west coast of Vancouver Island, near Tofino. So we went trolling and that's where I caught the biggest salmon... well, *we* caught it. I think he made me do most of the work. I can always brag about hauling in a sixty-nine-pound King. At that time they were paying ten cents a pound for salmon, two cents a pound for white King. The old man says, "No, we keep that one, take it home and smoke it." That was 1920.

In 1921, I went to Japan with a baseball team from Suquamish and two men from Seattle, Bill Rose and Johnny Lukonovik. A promoter named Moscow, that's what we called him, organized a series of games in different towns over there for us. He traveled with us until we got to Osaka, then he disappeared. Nobody ever found out where he went. We kept playing as best we could, promoting games for ourselves, first with the Japanese team from Osaka, and then with the Hawaiian All-Stars, who were on a tour there also. Art Sackman and I were sitting in a beer parlor one day, sipping our beer, and this Japanese tailor came over and wanted to talk. We could understand his English pretty well, and he asked us what we were doing. So we told him our sad story. He got in touch with the American Consul and paid the fare to Kobe for Johnny Lukonovik and me to talk to him. The Consul arranged for us all to get boat passage and four days later we were on our way home.

We got back in the fall, and that spring I went back to work in the woods and stayed there until the Depression, 1929, when we all got laid off. I had been working up around Snoqualmie, then, and I came home and started digging clams and beach seining. Jefferson Head was the favorite spot. I did that and worked at odd jobs around Indianola... carpentry, cutting wood... until the Second World War started. I managed to get back to the woods in 1956 and logged until I retired.

The museum that we have now will help the younger people see who was ahead of them. If they get any idea at all who the people were ahead of them, they're going to learn it there, because so many of them don't really know now. Boarding schools are just about a thing of the past. Now the Indian kids can go into the public school on an equal footing with the rest of them. If they don't get an education and get something going for themselves, though, it's going to be tough. I hope they are as tough as it is.

I've had a pretty good time all the way through, even with all the hard work. There has been some progress for us. I wish *I* could start over! And I'm not going to say I'd do it different. I'd probably do the same damn thing and have fun doing it! But where I got caught before, I'd probably get away with it now!

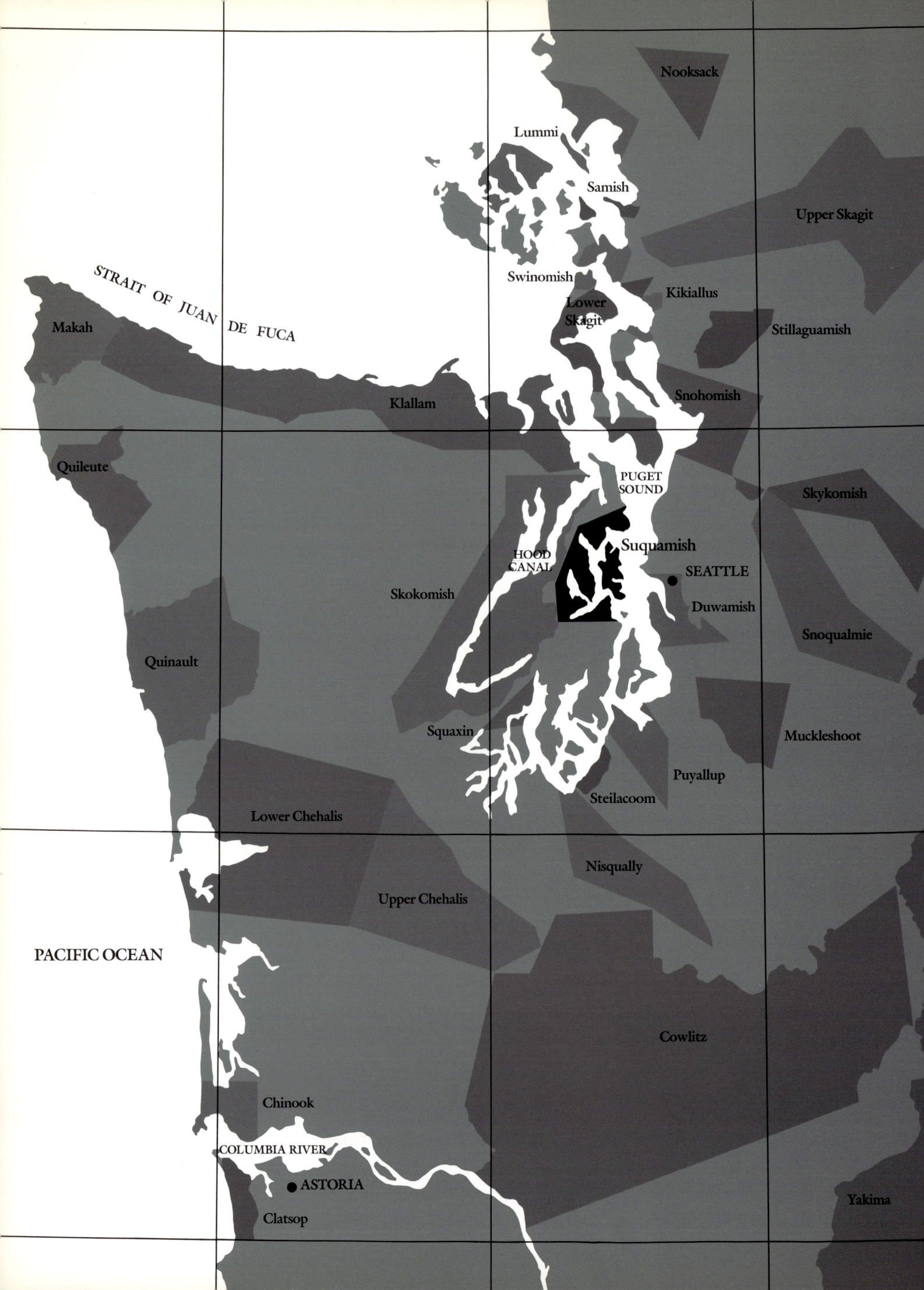

The Indians of Puget Sound

The Suquamish and their ancestors have inhabited the Puget area for thousands of years. Before the coming of the white man, this region was one of the most populated centers north of what is now Mexico City. Unlike the larger tribes of British Columbia, Alaska, the Plains, and the Southwest, the Indians of Puget Sound lived in relatively small, autonomous villages. Many tribes were affiliated through intermarriage, political agreement, trade, material culture, and language.

The abundance of natural resources and an efficient technology for harvesting and preserving food enabled them to develop a rich cultural and spiritual life. The yearly cycle of activities was divided between the harvesting of food from temporary camps in the warm months, and communal life in substantial winter houses for social and religious observances and protection against cold weather.

It was in 1792, three hundred years after Columbus landed in the New World, that the original inhabitants of the Puget Sound region gained their first direct knowledge of the white man. The American Revolution had just resulted in the birth of the United States, the French Revolution was in full swing, and the Industrial Revolution was beginning.

Rumors of strangers in odd sailing craft had been arriving for ten years from Indians further north and west toward the Pacific. Now Captain George Vancouver and the men of the British ship *Discovery* had come to map the Puget Sound in preparation to claim British ownership. They recorded, over a two-week period, evidence of habitation from Whidbey Island south to what is now Olympia. The various groups of Indians on Puget Sound treated the strangers in a equal manner, trading them fresh venison, fish, native berries and roots for beads, cloth, and iron.

Events during the years following Vancouver's visit greatly disrupted the traditional way of life. Diseases, such as smallpox, to which the Indians had no resistance, reduced the population of some areas by as much as eighty percent. Permanent white establishments—beginning with the Hudson Bay Company post at Nisqually in 1833 and in the Puget Sound area in the 1840s—reduced the tribes' fishing, hunting, and gathering sites. The treaties of 1855 grouped Indians onto reservations and many of the communal winter homes were destroyed.

In his famous speech to the Treaty Commission, Chief Seattle expressed a commitment to peace, but his final words indicated that he feared the end of his people and their way of life. Yet the native people of Puget Sound had survived for generations by adapting to their environment in efficient and complex ways. The people whose faces you see in this book survived the difficult one hundred years between 1855 and 1955 by adapting old skills and acquiring new ones.

Today the Suquamish, Duwamish, Muckleshoot, Skokomish, Nisqually, Snoqualmie, Puyallup, Snohomish, and other tribes are entering a period of renewed hope for the future. Tribal enterprises are being created in order to gain financial independence. Cultural centers have been established where tribal elders can pass on their knowledge of language, traditional skills, and religious customs.

Chief Seattle passed away in 1866. From his grave on the Kitsap Peninsula the modern city of Seattle is visible across Puget Sound. Knowing some of the early settlers as well as he did, the fact that the small village bearing his name survived and flourished would not surprise him. That his people have survived the challenges of this century would please him.

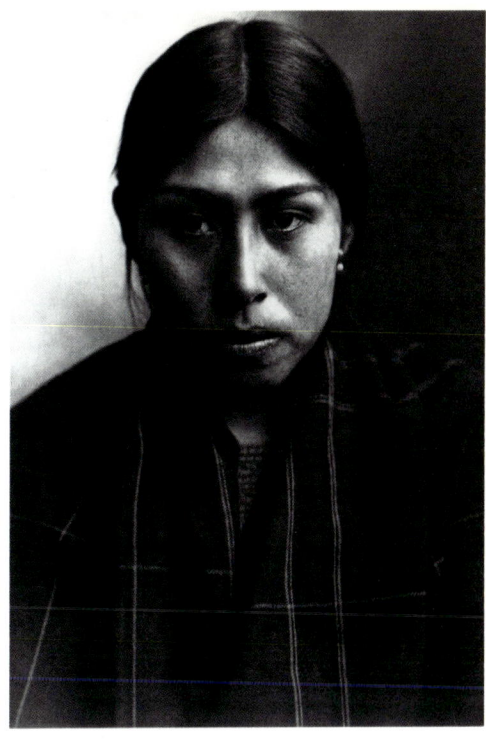

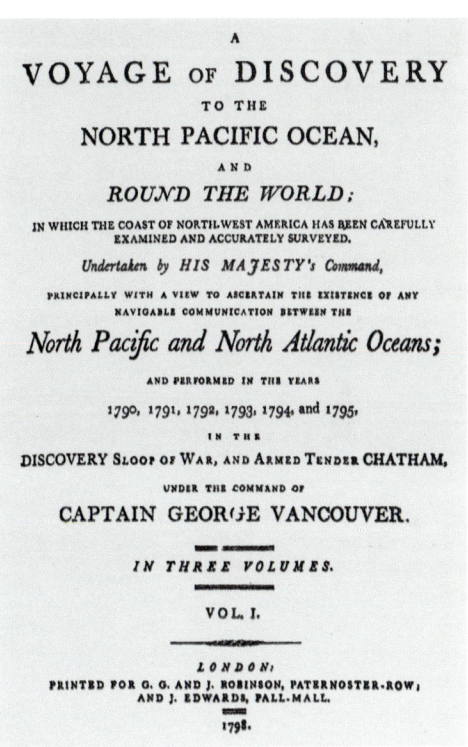

Upper, Suquamish Woman, E. S. Curtis. *Lower*, title page from Captain George Vancouver's *Voyage of Discovery*.

When they have a celebration or a big get-together, why Indians from all over come around. Some of 'em come by horseback, some of 'em come by canoe. Canada used to send down quite a few canoes. Great big ones, they'd load up, come across the waters and come down here. The Indian traveled all over, they didn't just stay in one little area all the time. —Earl Peck

Winter Dwellings and Lifestyle

The Indians of Puget Sound lived in permanent villages along the shore or near rivers and streams, with rectangular houses facing the water. These villages consisted of large wooden houses, called longhouses, which were often shared by many families. Longhouses were made of cedar planks and logs and had shed or gabled roofs. They varied in size with some of the larger structures ranging from two to six hundred feet long. They were divided into individual rooms, which opened to the outside.

Villages often had a potlatch house where people gathered for celebrations and ceremonies. The winter season was a time when elders instructed the young and traditions were passed on through song, dance, and storytelling. Activities such as carving, weaving, basket making, net making, and repair also took place during these months, as the community prepared for the coming fishing and gathering season.

Skirts, hats, and capes were woven of softened cedar bark and used as protection against the rain. In the only existing photograph of Chief Seattle, he is holding such a hat. The spindle and whorl were used to spin yarn composed of mountain sheep wool, duck down, and fireweed fluff, which was then woven into capes and blankets on a simple loom. Closely woven cattail mats were used as partitions and floor covering in the large winter houses, and as the covering for temporary summer dwellings.

Stone-bladed adzes were used to finish canoes after they had been roughed out of single logs with fire. Stone mauls and antler wedges were used to split cedar boards for houses. Smaller stone tools were used to butcher fish and game. Pierced and grooved stones were also used as canoe anchors and to weight fish lines and nets made of nettle-root twine. Metal replaced stone in many of these applications with the coming of the European explorers.

My earliest recollection of living in the village in the first five or six years of my life and the children were always playing there and the village run for about a mile along the shore of Suquamish. There's where we always seemed to gather, elders and children, sometime through the day . . . and the life of the people at that time wasn't too complicated . . . get up and do whatever chores or work they had to. —Lawrence Webster

Upper left, group at Old Man House Village on Agate Pass. *Upper right*, young Muckleshoot girl in traditional cedar bark clothing, bark shredder. *Lower left*, northern Puget Sound longhouse. *Lower right*, Chief Kitsap's family, from early tintype photograph.

Children The communal lifestyle of the Salish people allowed ample time for interaction between children, adults, and elders. Almost every activity in daily life could involved any age level. Evidence of the importance of molding children's play into learning activity exists in the art of work and play tools. Children's berry baskets with miniature tumplines were skillfully and lovingly prepared with small hands in mind. Children would accompany women during the berry harvest, with their small baskets in hand, and juice dripping from their chins as proof that they ate most of their harvest. While basket dolls were sought after as trade items by whites, they are another example of the loving care that parents and grandparents put into producing toys for their young.

Cedar Bark The most essential gift given to the Puget Sound Salish tribes is the Western Red Cedar. The entire tree is generous with its uses. Just the bark alone had numerous applications for everyday and ceremonial life.

During the winter months the raw inner bark of the cedar would take the shape of endless types of household, canoe, camp, and religious items. Usually, the bark would be beaten with a bark shredder to soften it and make it pliable. The beating process was long and tedious. The inner bark was laid over a sharp edge, such as a canoe paddle, and chopped with a bone or hardwood shredder with a scissors-like motion. After this, the bark was soft enough to be used as a newborn's diaper or an elder's towel.

Other bark products were: rope of all gauges, fish nets, skirts, capes, hats, baskets, mats, headdresses, decoration for masks, rattles, string, cradle padding, and canoe bailers.

Cedar bark was gathered in May or June when the sap was running and the tree loosened its grip. An ideal tree was of medium size with few or no lower branches. An incision was made near the bottom of the south side of the tree, just large enough for both hands to grasp. With a careful pull, the bark was peeled off in a slightly tapering ribbon. As the tear got higher on the tree, the harvester backed away and finished the separation with a swift jerk. The peeled bark had two layers, inner and outer, with the inner being the usable part. The two were separated by folding over one end of the long strip. This provided a start to separate the entire length. On a good day, only a few bundles of separated inner bark were hauled to the village for later use.

There was really no schooling as we know it today. What they taught 'em was how to survive. Of course, as far as teaching, learning, and what white man calls an education now, there was no method of that. You just had to live by the old Indian culture. Hunt, fish, whatever you can get in the resources there was around here. The elders, learned it from the elders. —Lawrence Webster

I've seen her prepare a complete meal in the sand. She'd make a bread at home an' she'd take and have it all prepared. An' she'd bury it in the sand, an' have a rock cod. She'd clean it and wrap it in seaweed and leaves and put it over there and build a fire over the top of it and go about her business. Noon time comes, go dig it up and it's already cooked. —Floyd Buber

Suquamish Villages

Traditionally, numerous Suquamish villages and camp sites were located throughout the Kitsap Peninsula, Bainbridge Island, Blake Island, and possibly the west side of Whidbey Island. The name "Suquamish" comes from the main village site along Agate Passage, called *d'suq'wub,* which means the place of "clear salt water."

In aboriginal times this village was a place of great concourse, where many Puget Sound tribes came together for trade and celebration. It was later the site of Old Man House, the largest longhouse on Puget Sound. This immense structure was not only the dwelling place of Chief Seattle and other Suquamish peoples, but also a major center for intertribal gatherings.

We kind of shared with one another. They didn't have but very little, but whenever they got anything they'd be one to share with you.—Ben George

Through the summer, I think most of the meals were right down there on the beach, 'cause there was always something doing. And when they had a big gathering down there and they were all bringing in clams to dry and one thing or another, after they'd get done with the day, they'd generally have a little pow wow, get-together, bone game, and start chanting some of their old songs until dark and then they'd go home.—Lawrence Webster

Large photo, Suquamish village at Eagle Harbor on Bainbridge Island. Insert photo, Salish summer camping site.

Food Gathering and Preparation

Choice game, fish, shellfish, and edible plants are plentiful in the Puget Sound area. Over the thousands of years of their occupancy here, native peoples developed an elaborate system for harvesting this abundance. During the warm summer months, the permanent winter villages of wooden houses were abandoned and temporary camps of houses made with poles and woven fiber mats were constructed near fishing, hunting, and gathering sites. Large canoes made of a single cedar log were used to transport people, lodgings, and the fruit of the harvest from place to place.

The variety of food gathered and preserved for winter by means of drying and smoking was impressive. Many species of berries, the tuber of cattails, two species of wild potato, onion-like bulbs of wild lilies, the roots of ferns, wild sunflower and dandelion, and several species of nuts were gathered in great numbers. These and a vast array of shellfish, including clams, oysters, shrimp, crabs, and mussels, were gathered and stored in the spring before the salmon runs began. Smoked and dried supplies were returned to the permanent winter sites for storage. The fishing harvest continued through fall. Villages were always situated near sources of food, such as shellfish, saltwater fish, and deer, that were readily accessible in the winter months. Marshlands were sites for hunting birds and waterfowl, as well as for gathering cranberries and Indian tea.

Meat and fish were either roasted on stakes by the fire or boiled by placing fire-heated rocks in tightly woven baskets filled with water. Certain vegetables and shellfish were steamed over hot rocks in pits. Hazelnuts and acorns were first cooked and then buried in mud for preservation. They were later washed and resoaked before eating. Camas, wild lily bulbs, and potatoes were stored. There is some evidence that the wild Indian potato, or wappato, may have been cultivated on a year-to-year basis. Some foods were eaten with salmon eggs or the new sprouts of plants including berries and ferns.

Daddy knew just what time of the year to kill a bear. And you can't tell the difference between it and beef. But if it's a time when they eat fish, their meat tastes bad. Time of the year when the berries are ripe, and the bears eat all berries, their meat is good and the fat on this is thick. —Clara Jones

Bowls and Spoons Meals were usually served in bowls or platters carved of alder and set on cattail mats. Each person dished out his or her portion with personal spoons carved of alder or made of the steamed and shaped horns of mountain goats, mountain sheep, and, later, domestic cows. Individual spoons were personalized by a carved or painted design and usually had a hole in the handle for a strap of cedar bark or leather.

Digging Stick These sticks were made of carefully seasoned ocean spray or yew wood and slightly tapered by carving both ends a bit. After carving, the points were fire-hardened for durability. When digging camas roots where more leverage was required, an extra handle of wood or antler was slipped onto one end. Women usually had three or four sticks of varying lengths for specific purposes. Shorter sticks were preferred for digging littleneck clams or roots that were closer to the surface. A large butter clam shell was often used with the stick to remove mud and sand. Longer sticks were used for horse clams and deeper roots and bulbs.

Berry Picker The berry picker is an easily made tool that allowed the user to whip red huckleberries off their branches and onto a mat in a fast and efficient manner. Other berries, such as blue huckleberries, were also gently raked off the branches and into a picking basket. The berries were then dumped into larger carrying baskets for the trip home, where they were usually dried as an important source of food for winter use. Berry pickers were made of ocean spray wood by first tying the middle of the stick with a cedar bark strap and then driving cedar wedges in above the wrap to split the tines open.

Squassom. They call it Indian ice cream. They just had to have squassom. Everybody used to make it their business to go down there to Discovery Bay. That's where they'd grow. Everybody used to sail and row down there in June and pick them while they're green. After they'd dry they'd soak half a cup of squassom berries in boiling water and let them sit until they's get soft and well up. They'd take them and put them in a bucket and take salal berry leaves and put them in your hand and hold it and stir, and you'd stir and stir until your bucket gets full. When it gets full you sugar it and if you like, you put jam in it. —Clara Jones

They used to dig the Swordfern roots. They're covered black, but they're white inside. They either toast it on a fire or boil them, they'd peel the black stuff off and eat just the inside. And they used to use that with fish or meat and it acted like potatoes. —Martha George

Large photo, William We-ah-lup (Tulalip) drying salmon and salmon eggs in the traditional manner. *Lower, left to right*, horn spoon, wooden bowl and spoon, wooden spoon, stone maul, wooden bowl and spoon, salmon club, clam digging stick, and berry picker.

19

Fishing

Before white settlement, fishing was the most important source of food for the Indians of Puget Sound. It remains today an important livelihood for many tribes. The Suquamish fished widely throughout Puget Sound, and continue to do so today.

A great deal of skill and knowledge was needed to determine when and where the various kinds of fish could be caught. The state of the tide, concentrations of birds and seals, the level of the water in streams, the weather, and other more subtle signs in the environment were all considered. Success in trade and sophisticated food preservation techniques permitted Puget Sound Indians to devote winter months to social gatherings and other activities.

Salmon were caught with nets, traps, or weirs, hook and line, and netting from canoes. Chinook, Coho, and Chum were the salmon most frequently caught in local waters. In addition, several kinds of trout were caught by these methods and other fish were caught with lures or speared. Lines and nets were made from nettle stems and roots.

Tidal impoundment traps were placed along the shoreline so that as the tide receded, fish were caught behind the weir, while water escaped. Puget Sound peoples commonly built fish weirs and various forms of traps in the shallow water of spawning streams and rivers. These consisted of tripods of sturdy poles held together by horizontal poles. Smaller sticks were tied to these poles to form a loose fence. The salmon, traveling upstream, were trapped and speared or taken with dip nets by men standing on platforms attached to the tripods. Ling cod and flounder were speared. Smaller fish, such as herring and smelt, were taken with "rakes."

Seals and porpoises, the most commonly hunted sea mammals, were taken with harpoons.

They'd make spears out of ironwood and they'd even put two points and sharpen the points. They'd tie it onto a long pole, I'd say eight or ten to twelve feet long, and then they could go out in deeper water to spear the fish with them. Sometimes they'd put three of those points on and they could catch smaller fish that way. On the spear points they'd have little notches on each of them, and that held the fish from slipping off... So easy with those notches on the points. —Martha George

Catching ducks... they'd drive poles out in the water on the beach. It don't have to be right at low tide, halfway down or better. So that the ducks would have to come inside of where these poles were, they'd stretch a mat net, anything that would block them when they went out. About the time the tide got high enough and the ducks were feeding, the water was up to the bottom of that net and if they got inside there, they'd scare the ducks out and they'd fly right out into the net and then they'd go gather them. The duck is something like a salmon. He can't go backward very well and he just keeps pushing into it. That's how they'd get 'em, right off the net. —Lawrence Webster

Large photos. *Left,* fishing for Chinook salmon with gill net; *right,* an Indian couple drying fish on racks. Insert photo, smoked salmon. *Lower, left to right,* halibut hook, oyster shell, clam shell, cockle shell, fish hook, toggling spear point, duck float, and herring rake.

Smoked Fish   Dried and smoked foods formed a large part of the Suquamish diet. Clams, salmon, salmon roe, berries, herring, and herring roe were the primary foods preserved by smoking. Smoked foods were always used in combination with fresh foods.

When salmon were running in certain creeks, families would set up camp at the site and build a smokehouse of branches, cattail mats, and cedar planks. (Smoking was also done in the longhouses.) Families stayed at the creek camps from two to eight weeks depending on the size of the fish run.

The Chum salmon shown here was sliced lengthwise and placed on sticks to keep it flat while it hung in the smokehouse. Alder wood and fir bark are used to create the smoke. After the fish was smoked it was hung in the longhouse rafters for winter, when it was boiled or eaten as is.

Halibut Hook   A spirit helper's strength was an advantage in catching this large, bottom-dwelling fish. Consequently, most hooks were adorned, as this one is, with a symbol of a spirit helper. The hook was baited, attached to a long line, and weighted near the bottom of certain uncommon deep holes in Puget Sound or out in the Strait of Juan de Fuca. The halibut sucks in everything in its path and spits out what is not acceptable. When it spits out the hook, the barb becomes lodged in its lip and its thrashing signals the fisherman above.

Toggle Point and Duck Float   This metal point was received in trade from non-Indians. In pre-contact times, similar points were made of bone, stone, or antler. The point would be slipped over the end of a harpoon shaft and a cedar bark rope connected the point to a float. When the prey was struck, the shaft fell away and the prey swam off dragging the float. The flat bottom of the float clapped against the surface of the water, helping the hunter locate the exhausted prey in the dark or fog. The duck-shaped float was occasionally painted with symbols of the hunter's spirit helper. Seal and other sea mammals were hunted by this method.

Herring Rake   The herring rake is a pole of cedar with a line of sharpened nails along one edge. Traditional rakes used sharpened pegs of bone or ocean spray wood (known to local Indians as iron wood) instead of nails. In pre-contact and early historical times, smelt or herring were swept into canoes with this remarkable tool. The user made a smooth semicircular sweep through the school of fish and with a continuation of the motion brought the fish up and shook them into the canoe. Smoked herring formed a significant part of the foods stored for winter and spring use.

The old man, he'd go out and hunt these porpoise that come around here. He'd barbecue 'em. He'd invite everybody around to come down and have some. He'd make a fire just like he was going to have a clambake, heating the rocks. He put seaweed or something between the layers of it. He'd have two or three layers of this steak he'd cut from the porpoise. —Ben George

So when we got tired eatin' everything else, he would go and kill a seal and we would eat seal. But you couldn't tell that from beef either—they boiled it and roasted it and fried it. —Clara Jones

Basket Making

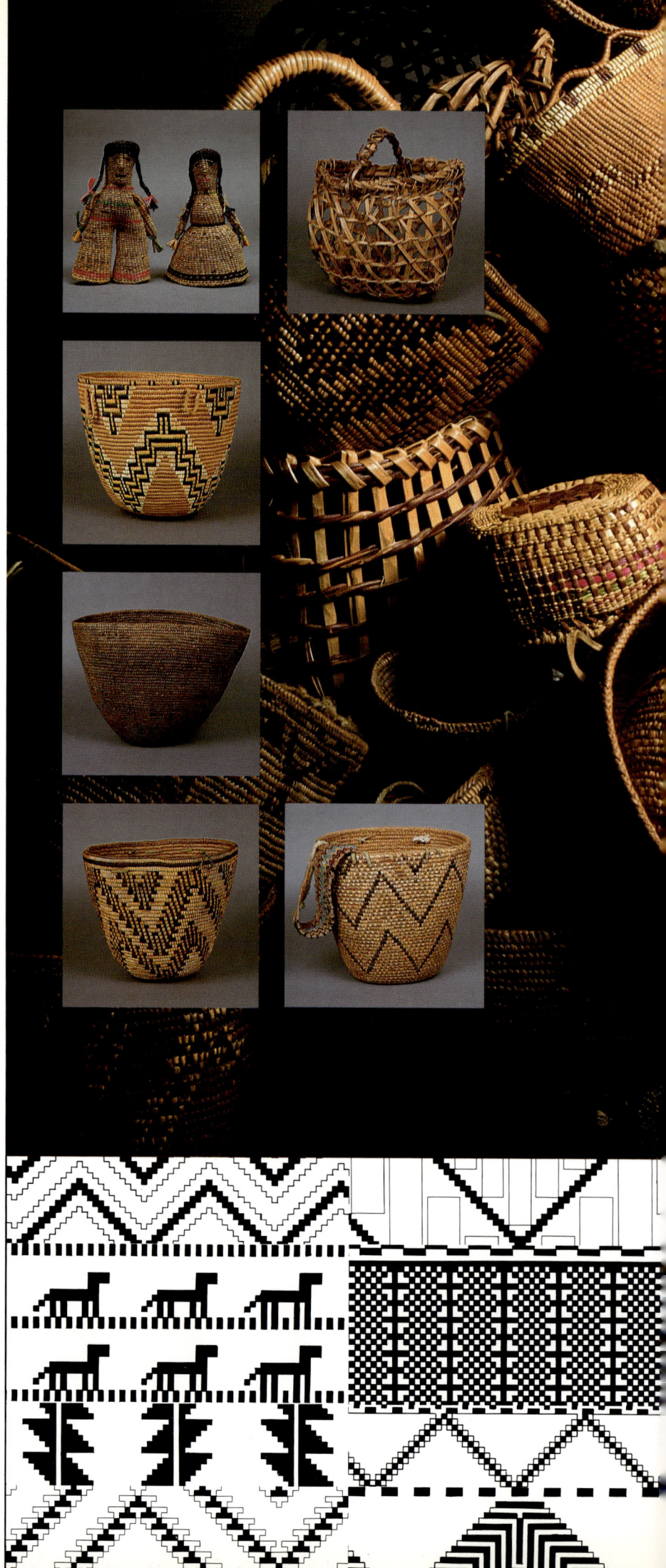

The complicated system of harvest, transport, and storage required making a great variety of baskets, each with a special use. Baskets were also woven as beautiful objects to be admired and given away to friends and relatives. Many were made specifically for trade with other tribes, or for sale as white settlers came to this area. Most basket making was done by women.

The coiled, or hard, basket was the most versatile of all containers made, and was considered the most valuable. It was used when picking berries, for carrying liquids, for storing dried foods, and for cooking. The open weave, twine "clam baskets" were useful for gathering clams, small fish, or seaweed. Roots and limbs of cedar were split into narrow strips to supply the raw material for such baskets. In coiled baskets some of these strips became the foundation for the wide horizontal coil, while others were used to sew the coil together with the aid of a sharp bone awl. Small strips of colored plant material, such as wild cherry bark, horsetail root, or dyed cedar bark, were sometimes folded under each stitch. This technique, known as imbrication, produced geometric patterns on the baskets. Twined baskets, like the Skokomish baskets in this book, were made with a vertical warp of twisted cattail fibers and two double-weft strands of both cattail and bear grass or some other decorative element.

I used to go with my grandmother once in awhile, gathering cedar roots or cedar limbs for basketry. The best place to look for them is in shady places, and I remember if there was an old rotten log, she used to go there and get all the roots from that tree. It would be all along, following the log. Sometimes those roots would be eighteen or twenty feet long. She used to take them and cut them up into about four-foot lengths and pack them down the beach. —Martha George

On my basketwork, I was just a little girl about seven years old when I first started to work... any waste, little work of my mother what she would throw away, I would pick up—just a little girl. I thought I had enough and I went outside and started work on it, started at the bottom. I made a little basket. From that time I kept on working and I'm still working on baskets. —Celia Jackson

It was my grandmother that taught me how to make baskets. She used to go out and get the cattails and go get the cedar bark and get cedar limbs to make clam baskets. She used to make me sit down and do it. She says, 'You got to learn how. You're goin' to get old, too, like I am, so you better learn how to make this.' —Ethel Sam

Clam Basket The clam basket was used to gather and transport small fish, shellfish, and other "beach" foods back to the village or camp. Since the Suquamish spent almost their entire life on Puget Sound or on the adjacent tidelines, the clam basket was the most commonly used basket.

Clams were the most important of these foods, since they were dug on a year-round basis and provided a constant supply of fresh food. Even in the winter, when the lowest tides were at night, clams were dug using torches of cedar bark and pitchwood. In spring, large quantities of littleneck clams, cockles, and horse clams were harvested and dried for later use or traded.

The clams were put into a small or medium-sized basket. Because of the open-weave construction, the clams were washed clean by simply shaking the basket underwater. The clams were then brought to the canoe and dumped into a large clam basket for transporting.

In spring and early summer, there was a large movement among all Puget Sound Salish tribes to the beaches of Puget Sound and Hood Canal to camp and to harvest and preserve large amounts of shellfish. Family and social alliances were important in the clam harvest, as it gave the more river-oriented tribes further access to clams and other beach foods. Visiting, trading, feasting, and socializing occurred during this period of the yearly cycle.

In making the clam basket, cedar root and cedar limbs were the most commonly used materials, although hemlock and spruce were sometimes utilized. Long, straight limbs and roots were most desirable. The best cedar roots were dug from trees growing on rotten logs, while the best limbs were taken in swampy areas. Both materials were split into sections, and the limbs were used for the main frame (warp) of the basket, while the root sections were used for wrapping (weft) to hold the basket together.

Clam baskets were heavily used, and were usually discarded after one season.

Berry Basket The smaller berry picking baskets would be filled by individuals and dumped collectively into this type of carrying basket. When full, this basket would be hoisted up on the back with the tumpline draped across either the shoulders or the forehead, and additional straps could be tied around the waist to keep the load from swaying.

The main construction material is cedar root. The design is a zigzag of horsetail root with all over "beading" of bear grass.

Hard Basket This type of basket would commonly be used to carry and hold drinking and cooking water.

Large photos. *Left*, Puget Sound baskets; *right*, Tennessee, a Suquamish basket maker, at her home at Port Blakely on Bainbridge Island. Insert photos, *from top to bottom, left to right*, basket dolls, Puyallup berry basket, Suquamish berry basket, coiled berry basket, clam basket, Suquamish berry basket, and small basket with three rows of animals. *Lower*, *left to right*, basket designs drawn by Pegie Ahvakana, basket-making materials, and basket maker.

Matting

The cattail was second only to the cedar tree in importance to the Suquamish and other Puget Sound Salish tribes. Baskets, rain clothing, and various styles of mats were made of this readily available material. A mat creaser, mat needle, and a good supply of cattails were all that was needed to make mats used for cushions and protective cover in canoes, to line walls, for sleeping, to serve meals on, and for housing.

The cattails for mats were gathered and processed in July or August, while they were tall but still not too dried out. Cattails were abundant throughout the Suquamish territory, but two favorite gathering spots were at the mouth of the Duwamish River and at two large marshes where the present city of Edmonds is located. The cattails were sun-dried, bundled up, and stored in the longhouse rafters until winter and early spring when the women had extra time to work on mats.

Mat Creaser This small hand-held tool, usually made of maple, takes the shape of a semicircle with a handle on top. The rounded bottom has a triangular groove cut in to fit over the mat needle. The upper edge is usually ornamented with carvings of birds or animals.

Mat needle This tool was used to impale the cattails at right angles and draw a string through them to hold the mat together. While the cattails were still impaled on the needles, the mat creaser was run over them. A set of three mat needles, made of ocean spray wood and about three feet long, were used in this process.

When the sap is running, they used to go out in the woods and peel the cedar bark and then they'd peel the outer bark and just save the inner bark, between the real bark and the tree. They made mats out of them and they made baskets out of them. They made a flat mat and wove it, and they'd use it as a tablecloth . . . they even used it to make their beds on next to the floor, then they'd put their blankets on it.—Martha George

Large photos. *Left, The Tule Gatherer*, E.S. Curtis; *right, Fishing Camp-Skokomish*, E.S. Curtis. Insert photos, details of various styles of matting. *Lower*, mat creaser, and two mat needles.

25

Weaving

Salish Blankets While Salish blankets were used for a warm covering at night, they also served as special symbols in ceremonies and considered valuable trade or gift items. A wealthy person gave numerous blankets away during a potlatch. In a naming ceremony, the recipient was "protected" by wearing a Salish blanket. Very small blankets were made to pad and wrap the infant in a cradleboard.

The abundance or scarcity of weaving materials were factors in determining the special versus ordinary blankets. Some spinning materials were mountain goat wool, wool from special dogs, and the down or feathers of the eagle, duck, or goose. "Filler" material consisted of stinging nettle fibers, the fluff of the fireweed plant, and possibly the catkins of the cattail plant. Over the years, sheep's wool replaced these and became the foremost spinning material.

Collecting and preparing the various materials were very time-consuming tasks. Sometimes the weaver traded for mountain goat wool or plucked bits of it from the bushes along mountain trails. Ducks or geese were caught in nets or shot with arrows, and the down was saved. The wool dogs were secluded by themselves, sometimes on islands, to keep them from breeding with the camp dogs. This allowed them to keep their long, woolly fur pure for shearing and spinning.

The next step in the process was to wash and pick the fibers clean of any impurities. Once dried, a certain swamp clay was sprinkled over the materials and beaten in with a sword-shaped stick. This served several purposes: beating fluffed the wool, the clay soaked up oils to make handling easier, and further cleaned the wool.

The spindle and spindle whorl varied in sizes depending on the desired yarn. A small heavier stone or bone whorl was used for fine yarn, while coarse yarn was spun on a larger lightweight whorl. Unlike the northern coast Salish tribes, no elaborately carved whorls have been found to date among the Puget Sound Salish.

The spinning was done by attaching a strand of wool to the whorl where it sits on the spindle, and then twirling the spindle by hand over the thigh. The strand was connected to the top of a pole high over the spinner's head. As the whorl spun, the strand was twisted until the appropriate gauge was reached. Length by length, the wool was spun in this fashion and then bound around the spindle into a ball.

The loom for weaving Salish blankets consisted of a sturdy frame of two cedar posts stuck deep in the ground, usually five feet apart, and two rollers carved out of hardwood. The rollers fit into slots in the cedar posts. To begin weaving, a straight stick was suspended halfway between the two rollers and secured. There were two types of warping techniques, the most common was reverse wrapping. When this complicated method was used, it allowed the weaver to simply pull out the suspended stick, letting the finished blanket fall free of the loom. No cutting or finishing of the edges was necessary, save for adding an optional fringe.

Weaving the blanket was done by hand, no shuttle was used and rarely was a heddle used. Elders who taught the craft, thought it unwise to depend upon too many tools, when your hands could do the precise work alone. There are conflicting historical accounts of techniques concerning direction of weave and use of a heddle.

Left, detail of a Salish blanket. *Right*, Salish weaving loom.

Canoes

Canoes The dugout canoe was an integral part of Suquamish culture. This craft was the major form of transportation: the heavily forested land made efficient foot travel difficult. The canoe was essential to the collection of subsistance resources, such as salmon and other fish, berries, roots, wild potatoes, and sea grasses. These foods were seasonal and regional, and the Suquamish needed to be in particular places at specific times in order to harvest them. The canoe allowed them to travel long distances in a relatively short time, assuring quantities of food, establishment and renewal of tribal alliances, and the preservation of social and ceremonial contacts, which in turn permitted the culture to flourish beyond mere survival.

A good canoe, made in the traditional manner usually took one year to complete. The canoe maker was trained in the art from an early age, usually with much practice in producing models and small one-person craft. Most men were capable of making a simple canoe but only the masters were able to make the larger versions successfully. The first step was to select the proper tree. It had to be straight and tall, have few branches, be near the water, be free of rot, and have a soft place to fall. Western Red Cedar and Yellow Cedar were the two suitable species: both are lightweight, hard, and preserve well due to their oiliness. The tree was fallen by either carving a notch at the base and burning the wood the rest of the way through, or by chiseling the base completely through. Next it was roughly shaped enough to allow transport to the beach near the village where detailed work took place. This was done with chisels and wedges struck with hand mauls. The canoe was turned upside-down and the hull was carved to perfection then turned over and hollowed out. Then it was filled halfway with water and hot stones in order to create steam to spread the sides. Cross sticks were used to keep them spread. Some tribes attached separate bow and stern pieces with cedar pegs, completing the fine lines and adding character to the finished product.

Large photo, camp on Ballast Island in Seattle. Insert photo, two Suquamish women in a cedar dugout canoe. *Lower, left to right*, canoe bow piece, two canoe paddles, anchor stone, canoe bailer, hand adze, three adze blades, and adze handle.

Paddles Traditionally, there were two main types of paddles for the Suquamish and Puget Sound Salish: the man's paddle and the woman's paddle. The man's type was longer although there were variations of each type. Some paddles were made with a wide blade to increase speed while others had a thinner, sharp blade for sticking into mud to anchor a canoe. The sharp blade was also used in warfare. Designs representing the owner's spiritual helper were painted on some paddles, usually with red ochre or black paint. Maple and yew wood were used in carving paddles, maple being the most common of these.

Anchor Stone Large anchor stones were used to secure the ends of fishing lines and nets or to anchor canoes off shore temporarily. Holes for tying were laboriously pecked in these stones with the use of smaller, harder stones. Success on a fishing trip might depend on the stability of a line or net. The anchor was an important tool that had to be cared for as it could not be easily replaced.

Canoe Bailer Three types of bailers were common to this region and were necessary tools for the canoe people of Puget Sound. One was fashioned from a rectangular piece of cedar bark. Wild cherry bark or inner cedar bark strips would be used to lash the bailer to a handle of dry, peeled limb. A bailer such as this would only take a few minutes to make, and had a short life span. Another other type of bailer also common on Puget Sound was carved out of cedar or alder and shaped like an upside-down pyramid. This bailer had a groove in the bottom for grasping, or an attached rope of cedar bark or root. A third type of bailer was carved out of alder or cedar in the shape of a large angular spoon.

At a certain time of the year, which was generally in August—I remember it from being a youngster—they'd gather over in Seattle, down on the flats, there. When I say flats, most people don't know where it is. That's nearly everything beyond or south of Yesler Way. Mud flats, cattails, one thing an' another. They'd get in there and do a little trading with the whites and also with some Indians.—Lawrence Webster

You'd go in a canoe where water's six or eight feet deep, and then you'd spear flounders or whatever kind of fish you'd see.—Martha George

Spiritual Life

In ancient times, the native peoples of Puget Sound had a living faith that was much more than a worship and respect for nature. They saw all of existence as alive and feeling, having the same range of thoughts and emotions as human beings.

In the very beginning, there was a wonderful world here long before human beings arrived. It was a world where everything had the power and ability to take any form or do anything. A world inhabited by beings who might appear as animals, plants, in human or inhuman form, or as aspects of the landscape, always shimmering between these and other shapes. Finally, a firm order was imposed on this world by The Changer, enabling human beings to take their place in the world.

As a result, the beings have been changed in the shapes of trees, plants, animals, fish, rocks, springs, and so forth, while their spirits retain their original abilities. In these forms, they have retained their full intelligence and emotions, and many have entered into partnerships with particular individuals to grant them abilities and careers.

As the most recent inhabitants of this world, human beings are believed to have the most to learn. Yet, such an education is possible because all of life is related, forming a functioning whole. Special powers and abilities can be approached through fasting, prayer, meditation, and rituals. Many parts of the old religion are still important in the lives of those who have incorporated Catholicism, Shakerism, and varieties of Christianity into their religious beliefs.

Traditional teachings still play an important role in the modern world. While participating in many of the same denominations as the rest of America and Europe, native peoples have nonetheless also maintained their special relationship with the land and with its sacred aspects. As the larger population becomes more aware of the virtues of being ecumenical, ecologically aware, and respectful of the limitations of our planet, the virtues of traditional respect for nature are becoming better appreciated, understood, and encouraged.

You want to leave things as they are and just take what you need. Don't be wasteful, that's what the elders taught. —Martha George

Large photos. *Left*, companion and Annie Rogers, *right*, group at blessing of Chief Sealth's grave during Chief Seattle Days. *Lower, left to right*, ceremonial headband, deer hoof rattle, hand drum and drum stick, bird rattle, and mask.

Drum and Drumstick Since a successful life for the Suquamish and other Coast Salish depended on the assistance of spiritual helpers, individuals had songs and dances to gain this help. For most of these, beating a rhythm was necessary. The hand drum served this purpose in winter ceremonies, gambling, doctoring, travel in canoes, or singing and dancing for pleasure.

During winter ceremonies, the rhythm sometimes came from beating on the longhouse rafters with a long pole. During Slahal gambling games, a pole was laid out in front of each side of players. The players beat on the pole with sticks while singing their songs.

Hand drums were square, round, or many-sided with a cedar root or cedar wood frame, and normally covered with deer hide. A handle was formed underneath by crossed and wrapped straps.

Bird Rattle Rattles were used in both public and secret ceremonies. Certain types of rattles were used for very specific purposes. Shamans used a special rattle for healing the sick. In this instance, the shaman is calling on the assistance of his spirit helper(s) for the power to heal. A leader in the community would use a large rattle to call together gatherings which always involve ceremony. Dancers used rattles in performing personal or family songs and dances, for spiritual purposes and to call on the aid of a spirit helper.

Although the sound of the rattle in concert with the melodic singing of the people was definitely music, the deeper meaning was communication to the spirit world.

Many types of rattles were made and used by the Puget Salish. Among them are duck-shaped rattles, deerhoof rattles, shell rattles, and this elegantly carved bird rattle.

This rattle was carved of wood and, while still in its rough shape, was split and the body was hollowed out. Pebbles were put inside and the rattle was tied shut.

Mask In the literature on the Puget Sound Salish, there is little mention of uses for masks like this. The nearest common and identifiable ones are the Skhwaikhwey masks of the northern coast Salish, and the humanoid masks and wolf headdress of the Makah on the west coast. There is mention only by Eells of masks being used in the black-faced ceremonies. In Puget Sound Salish society, though, much of what was painted or carved on common or ceremonial objects had to do with special spirit helpers who directed the form that the decoration takes. Cooperation with spirit helpers by use of these designs gained the helpers' support on special or ceremonial occasions. This mask was owned by Sam Snyder, a traditionally raised Suquamish, who was said to have strong personal spiritual helpers.

Necklace The large necklace made of Chinese coins, blue glass Hudson Bay Company trade beads, and dentalia shells colorfully illustrates the trade system that was once the primary foundation of tribal alliance throughout the region. Although items such as glass beads and Chinese coins are indicative of non-Indian trade relations, a full and complete trading system was in place long before white invasion. Adornment trade items included beautiful shells and shell fragments. Horn, antler, bone, and wood all served to embellish the individual.

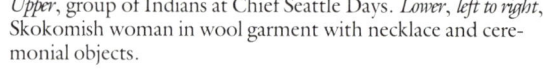

Upper, group of Indians at Chief Seattle Days. *Lower, left to right*, Skokomish woman in wool garment with necklace and ceremonial objects.

Tribal Alliances and Trade

The Suquamish Tribe participated in an extensive network of alliances in pre-contact times. The alliances made among tribes were secured through marriage. In addition to mutual defense, tribes obtained economic benefits from trade and exchanges of ideas. Food baskets, mats, blankets, canoes, and raw materials were basic to the economic structure of the area. Each group had an overabundance of specific commodities for trade: the Suquamish had dried clams, the Makah had whale products, and the Snohomish had deer or bear meat. Extensive travel was necessary for these transactions, so long visits would usually begin with a meal in the evening and soon turn to singing, gambling, and dancing. These were times to meet new people, make new friendships, and to look for prospective husbands and wives. In more recent times, these gatherings occurred during seasonal trips to work sites, such as when hop picking south of Seattle. The Chief Seattle Days celebration at Suquamish is an example of the practice continuing to the present day.

Slahal Bones Bone cylinders were used to play the traditional gambling game called "Slahal." The object of the game was for one team to guess the position of the unmarked bones. The team holding the bones hid them in their hands covered by a hat or a blanket. The team trying to guess the whereabouts of the unmarked bones was further confused by their opponents who sang songs of praise for themselves and shame for the guessing team. Both teams wanted to win the "purse," an equal bet placed by each team before the game began. Slahal games sometimes lasted several days and usually matched two tribes or villages against each other. Traditionally only men played this game.

I can remember about the hop field—they'd pick through the day but every evening there was a bone game and songs going on. I don't know who was winning all the money or losing it or if they were playing for money or not, they'd have it just about every evening. So I sometimes wonder if it wasn't just more for pleasure than anything else—to get away from those ordinary run of things. Nobody ever seemed to come home rich. It was a chance to get out and enjoy themselves, I guess. Could have been economically good for some of them, but there was an awful lot of them that didn't seem to care whether they made any money or not. —Lawrence Webster

Upper, trolling for salmon in a saltwater canoe. *Center*, Suquamish Indians working in hop fields. *Lower left*, Indian group gambling on a beach near Tacoma. *Lower right*, gambling bones and discs.

The Treaties and Their Aftermath

In 1854, several years after white settlers began to establish themselves in the Puget Sound area, the United States government elected to make treaties with Indians in what was then known as Washington Territory. The treaties were necessary to extinguish title to land in order to free it for white settlement. The treaties were legal contracts negotiated between equals: the sovereign Indian governments on the one hand and the United States on the other.

In the treaties, tribes relinquished claims to most of the land they occupied and at the same time reserved a number of smaller "reservations" near their winter village sites. Indians also reserved the right to continue to hunt, gather, and fish without interference in traditional areas off their reservations. In exchange for all of the ceded Indian lands, the federal government agreed to provide limited supplies, educational services, and modest monetary compensation. The government also agreed to protect Indian rights and lands that were reserved to the tribes.

The Suquamish was one of more than twenty tribal groups that were parties to the Treaty of Point Elliott, signed near Mukilteo, on north Puget Sound, on January 22, 1855. This document was the second of five treaties which Territorial Governor Isaac Stevens negotiated with tribes in western Washington. Accompanying Stevens were lawyer/ethnologist George Gibbs, who was surveyor and Secretary for the Treaty Commission; Michael T. Simmons, Indian Agent for the Puget Sound District; Benjamin Shaw, the interpreter; and witnesses. Representing both the Suquamish and Duwamish tribes at the treaty signing was Chief Seattle, along with many subchiefs and leaders of other tribes. The Indians far outnumbered the Stevens entourage, just as the Indians out numbered white settlers at the time.

The negotiations were conducted in Chinook, a limited trade jargon taken from the French, English, and Indian languages. Many Puget Sound people did not speak this concrete shorthand language of a few hundred words, which was adequate for trading goods but not for legal negotiations. Therefore, the treaty was first read in English, translated into Chinook jargon, and then into two languages of the Coast Salish stock—Lushootseed and Straits Salish. Given the limitations of the jargon and the fact that the concept of land alienation was unknown to the Indians, the language problem produced difficulties in translation. Also, the treaties were made in great haste because Governor Stevens was anxious to negotiate all of the treaties as soon as possible. Together these circumstances created misunderstandings which persist to this day.

The Port Madison Indian Reservation was reserved in the Treaty of Point Elliott and was intended primarily for the use of Suquamish and Duwamish peoples. Most of the Suquamish agreed to move to the reservation, which was located within their own territory. However, a number of Suquamish families chose to remain in villages at nearby locations such as those at Elwood, Erland's Point, Colby, Chico, Phinney Bay, and Bainbridge Island.

While some Duwamish people moved to the Port Madison Reservation, many others declined to relocate and asked that a separate reservation be set aside in their own homeland, located where the Black and Cedar rivers joined, near the present city of Seattle. The Muckleshoot Reservation was enlarged in hopes that the Duwamish would move to that area.

The treaties were not ratified by Congress until four years following negotiations, during which time many of their provisions were being violated. Disputes over land ownership, reservation rights and boundaries, and fishing rights have arisen frequently since then. Seven times the United States Supreme Court has addressed issues involving the reserved right to fish in off-reservation waters. Each time the Court has substantially affirmed the tribes' treaty rights. Some disputes are still awaiting court decision today, 130 years after the signing of the treaties. The treaties reserved to the tribes certain rights with regard to self-government. This pledge of Indian self-determination has been supported over the years through major congressional action.

Upper, treaty protest at Olympia, 1864. *Center and lower*, excerpt and signatures from Point Elliott Treaty.

Chief Seattle's Speech

In reality, there were no hereditary chiefs among the Puget Sound Indians. Strong leaders arose in each village from time to time who, distinguishing themselves by their actions or particular skills, were respected and followed. For instance, there were fishing leaders, peacetime leaders, and leaders in times of crisis. Seattle was one of these. In addition to his leadership skills and his ability to understand what the white settlers' intentions were, he was also a noted orator in his native language. At the presentation of the treaty proposals in 1854, Chief Seattle delivered a magnificent speech, which is widely remembered today. It is the speech of a man who had seen his world turned upside-down in his own lifetime: as a boy he had seen Vancouver's ships, and when he died the treaty protests were still going on. The following is the last part of his speech, translated by Dr. Henry Smith, a Salish speaker and, according to some sources, an eyewitness.

We will ponder your proposition and when we decide we will let you know. But should we accept it, I here and now make this condition—that we will not be denied the privilege without molestation, of visiting at any time the tombs of our ancestors, friends and children. Every part of this soil is sacred, in the estimation of my people. Every hillside, every valley, every plain and grove, has been hallowed by some sad or happy event in days long vanished. Even the rocks, which seem to be dumb and dead as they swelter in the sun along the silent shore, thrill with memories of stirring events connected with the lives of my people, and the very dust upon which you now stand responds more lovingly to their footsteps than to yours, because it is rich with the dust of our ancestors and our bare feet are conscious of the sympathetic touch. Our departed braves, fond mothers, glad, happy-hearted maidens, and even the little children who lived here and rejoiced here for a brief season, still love these sombre solitudes and at eventide they grow shadowy of returning spirits. And when the last Red Man shall have perished, and the memory of my tribe shall have become a myth among the white man, these shores will swarm with the invisible dead of my tribe, and when your children's children think themselves alone in the field, the store, the shop, upon the highway, or in the silence of the pathless woods, they will not be alone. In all the earth there is no place dedicated to solitude. At night when the streets of your cities and villages are silent and you think them deserted, they will throng with the returning hosts that once filled them and still love this beautiful land. The White Man will never be alone.

There is much discussion about the accuracy of this translation. Many people believe that it was embellished with phrases that were not truly Seattle's. Nevertheless, the overall theme and the depth of its meaning are clearly reflected. Seeing, however briefly, the land we live in through the eyes of Chief Seattle, is a fitting tribute to this eloquent leader and the will of his people to survive.

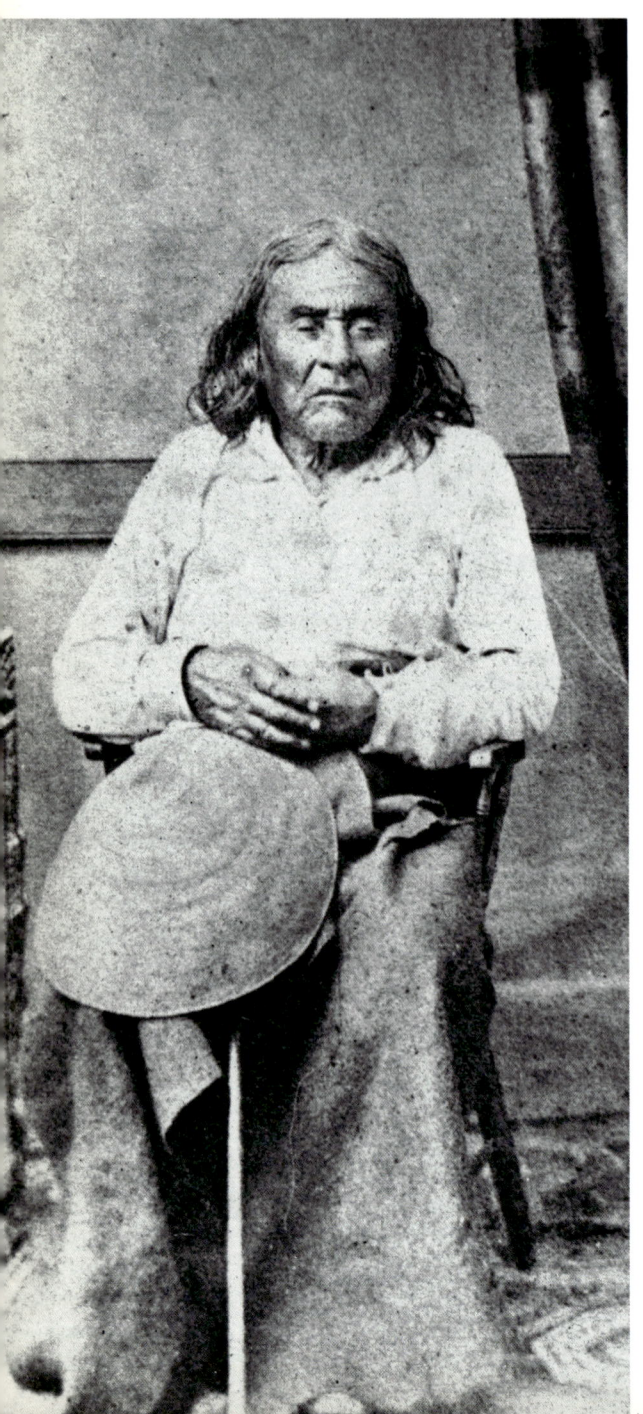

Opposite page, *left to right*, Chief Seattle; Angeline, daughter of Chief Seattle; and Jim Seattle, son of Chief Seattle. *From top to bottom*, welcoming dance at Chief Seattle Days, procession dance at Chief Seattle Days, and Chief Seattle Day buttons.

The Advent of Reservation Life

They took you off to school, and while you got white man education there you lost what you could have learned at home. I don't begrudge the going to school, but I almost lost the Indian language, to boot. I lost that much time away from home with those long winter evenings when they used to tell us the stories and one thing and another. —Lawrence Webster

The beginning of reservation life marked a significant transition in Suquamish history. Federal agents were assigned to take charge of the reservation, despite the existence of strong tribal leadership. In the decades following the Treaty of 1855, the federal government made gradual attempts to put an end to the traditions and communal lifestyle of the Suquamish people. Certain ceremonies and religious practices were outlawed at this time. Additionally, in the 1870s the acting federal agent at Port Madison ordered the burning of Old Man House at Agate Pass, the physical and spiritual heart of the Suquamish community.

During the following years, families continued to live in the village surrounding this site. At the turn of the century, the village included over thirty-five homes, a Catholic church, a schoolhouse, smokehouses, and several orchards. Village life was further disrupted when, in 1905, the United States War Department acquired nearly fifty acres of this land for a proposed military post. Houses were uprooted, as were the schoolhouse and church. Those having to move were paid twenty-four dollars apiece. Each family was to move to an individual parcel of land, or allotment, on the reservation. Suquamish leaders, concerned for their traditional homeland and the dispersal of their people, agreed to move from the village and, according to tribal elders, with the understanding that the property would return to the tribe if no longer needed for military purposes. Although a military post was never established, the land did not return to tribal possession.

From 1886 to 1910, land allotments were made on the reservation according to a provision in the Point Elliott Treaty. This action paralleled federal policy aimed at creating independent family farmsteads. The government hoped to replace traditional ways with those of white society by encouraging ownership of private land and farming among Indians. Yet the Suquamish were able to farm very little, as the land was poorly suited for such purposes, maintaining instead their fishing and hunting lifestyle. An allotment owner was expected to clear, develop, and otherwise "improve" his land, or risk losing it. These allotments were scattered throughout the reservation, often covered by dense forests far from the shore, a primary source of food.

Some families homesteaded lands off the reservation because an insufficient number of allotments were created. Others chose to remain in traditional off-reservation villages, and tried to acquire land through homesteading.

Upper left, St. George's Mission School on the Puyallup Indian Reservation. *Upper right*, Father F. Chirouse and his Indian students at Tulalip.

Indian Boarding Schools

From the 1880s through the 1920s, the federal government made an intensive effort to assimilate Indian people into white society by attempting to eliminate the cultural heritage of Indian youth, and replace it with non-Indian values. Thus began the policy of removing children from their families and sending them to Indian boarding schools off their reservations. Many industrial schools were established to supplement or replace those boarding schools already started by missionaries.

Together with children from other tribes across the nation, Suquamish children attended schools near Tacoma and Everett in Washington, as well as schools in Oregon and California. Today tribal elders remember the schools with mixed feelings. Some feel that the strict discipline, academic studies, and job skills helped prepare them for later life. Yet many students, particularly women, expecting to receive a useful education found themselves instead serving an economic function in the daily operation and maintenance of the schools.

Being removed from their home communities and prohibited from practicing cultural traditions was a great hardship. Tragedy struck several schools in western Washington when epidemics of whooping cough, measles, and other communicable diseases took the lives of countless children, who were concentrated together in one place and had no natural immunity to such diseases of the white man.

By the late twenties, a movement had begun to reform Indian education. By this time many Indian children were attending public schools with non-Indians. Even today, however, many Indian youth attend boarding schools in some areas of the United States where there is a lack of adequate schools near reservations.

You take any nationality there is, take them away from home, put 'em with a different group altogether, stay there for quite a number of years, he's going to forget a lot that he learned at home. And I don't care who it is, he's going to forget some things altogether. And if he's taken away very young from that home, he'll lose it just that much faster. —Lawrence Webster

Left, Lena and Clara Siddle, Tulalip Indian School. *Right, from top to bottom*, line-up of boys at the Cushman Trade School, house boys, kitchen girls, Cushman Trade School Band at Point Defiance Park in Tacoma.

All of a sudden, why, my folks... broke the news to us that we were to go to this school because there wasn't any schools around here. And that we had to go.... Mother didn't like it very well, but she said it just had to be done, that's all there is to it. I didn't even know anything about it. I felt bad when we was goin'... along come a boat, a big motor boat... anchored out here and picked us up. Like little cows, we got in and away we went. We didn't even know where Tulalip was or anything ... and at the end of the year, they'd bring us back. Next year, same thing.—Woody Loughrey

We stayed there [Cushman] for three years. We were just kids, you know. They [parents] said we had to go or else they would go to jail. That's what they used to tell us. And we would cry, 'We don't want to go back, we don't want to leave home.' They would tell us you will have to go or else we go to jail. There were some around two, three, four, five years old. They had these long rooms for our girls and there was sometimes forty to fifty beds in one room.—Clara Jones

There was a man used to come around pick us up every year the school started and take us off. And we'd stay there till school was out. And lots of time we never came home, we stayed, and we worked. I used to work out in Everett during the summertime in the fruit cannery.—Josephine Sparks

Death was about the only way you could get home. You were practically locked up for those nine, ten months. It had to be a sickness or death before they'd let you out of there very long.—Lawrence Webster

I used to cook so much for the Shaker meetings after I growed up, and I thought, 'Well, I'm going to go to this boarding school, and maybe I'll learn something else.' Do you know that when I got there, they just throwed me right into the kitchen work again. And, oh brother, I thought I was getting away from the kitchen work.—Ethel Sam

I think Cushman was more beneficial to the children than it was at Tulalip because you had a chance if you wanted to learn anything about machinery or tailoring or something, you had a chance to learn it there.—Lawrence Webster

They tried to give us an education by sending us to school and at the same time they tried to take your culture away from you by not letting you talk your own language.... All we did was talk Indian until I went to school, and then I had to learn how to talk English.—Lawrence Webster

I wouldn't even notice I'd say something in Indian, and then the teacher'd come along with his ruler and hit me on the hand, 'You talk English'.... The teachers used to scold us. Sometimes they'd think that we're talking about 'em.—Ethel Sam

It [Tulalip] was like a military school. You lined up and marched, to almost everything you did. And boy, you toed the mark. You know it was just like you was in the military—all the little kids, right down to the smallest one. They had companies—Company A and B. You lined up ... by bugle calls, just like the Army ... and then they had marching competition—the girls and boys. And by God, we couldn't beat those girls.—Woody Loughrey

Changes in Land Ownership

Although the Treaty of Point Elliott of 1855 provided that the Port Madison Reservation be held "in trust" for the tribe by the federal government, pressure rapidly increased for sale of these lands. Logging companies were interested in the timber, and entrepreneurs looking for investment property were attracted to the reservation's proximity to Seattle and pleasant surroundings. Therefore, almost immediately after land was allotted, the Indian owned property began to diminish.

Although some Indians chose to sell their land, much was sold without the owner's consent by federal agents who deemed the Indian owner "non-competent." Based on a federal act of 1907, agents were empowered to declare Indians "non-competent" if, for example, they could not speak English or lacked a monetary income. Three years later, legislation was passed granting agents the power to give "certificates of competency" to Indians, which resulted in the removal of land from federal trust status. Relying on a fishing and hunting subsistence, many tribal members were unable to pay the state taxes subsequently imposed on their land, and were forced to relinquish their property.

Today, a large percentage of reservation lands are owned by non-Indian residents. A major goal for the tribe has been to purchase land on the Port Madison Reservation for the benefit of the Suquamish community. The recent establishment of a tribal housing development has enabled many Suquamish people, who have otherwise not been able to do so, to move back to the reservation.

Large photo, Suquamish Indians awaiting a steamer to return them to Bainbridge Island, after attempting to collect their payments for land bought by the government. *Lower, left to right*, real estate advertisements for Chief Seattle Park.

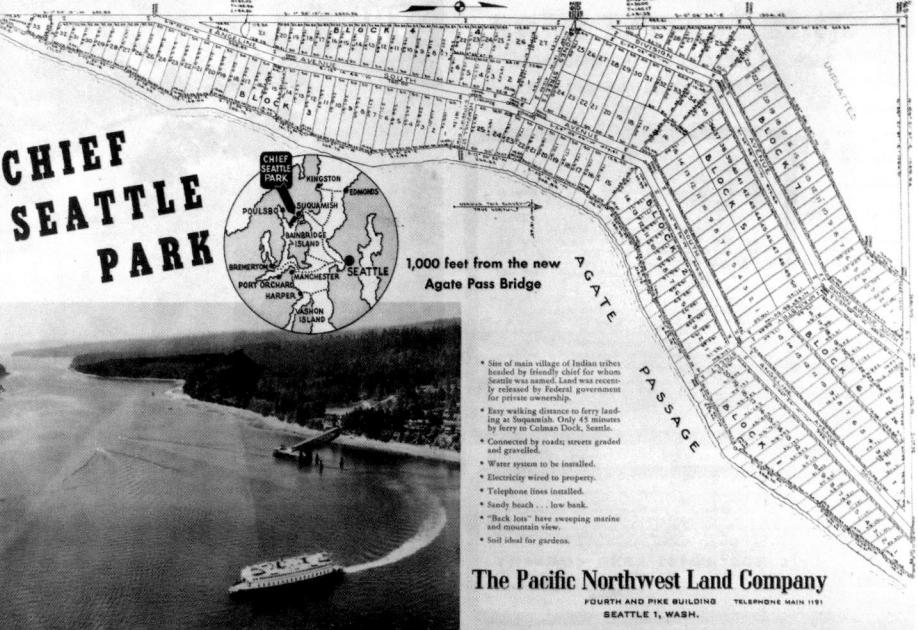

Transition in Labor and Economy

From first contact with western European culture, Puget Sound peoples engaged in a lively system of trade with non-Indians. For a short time during initial settlement the immigrants depended on Indian goods for survival. They acquired dugout canoes for transportation, split cedar board houses for shelter, Indian baskets for food gathering and storage, and dogfish oil to grease the skid roads used for logging. Indians traded these items, as well as salmon and shellfish, in exchange for manufactured goods, which they incorporated into their technology and culture.

As the larger society diversified and became more complex, the occupations of Suquamish people also expanded to meet the needs of the era. Many Indian men and women played a significant role in the local labor force by marketing fish and shellfish and by working in logging camps, sawmills, hopfields, shipyards, and defense industries. The need for monetary income to supplement the increasingly depleted and inaccessible fisheries and forest resources, coupled with changing expectations, caused many Suquamish to seek seasonal employment off the reservation. Nevertheless, most maintained permanent residence within the tribal community.

Hard work and perseverance have long been survival skills of the Suquamish people. For this reason, they were able to make major adjustments to a foreign culture while at the same time continuing their traditional hunting, fishing, and gathering.

Logging. In those days it was dangerous. You could break your back or lose your leg or your arm, something like that... safety measures. Ain't everybody that's fast enough to get out of the way of a tree when it's falling down.—Bernard Adams

Indians always worked. They worked at the logging camps and worked at the Gamble mill.—William Pickrell

And the clams... in those days, right after the Depression, if you had a contract with the market, say for three sacks on Monday, three sacks on Wednesday, and maybe four or five on Friday, that meant just what they said. Because there was plenty of people waiting in line to grab that job if you once slipped up. We never had any trouble with the markets.—Bernard Adams

I went to work for the government—I will never forget this date—it was the 29th of May, 1940, and I got into Keyport and I got on a permanent list the same year in November of that year, and I stayed with it. I started right on the bottom as a laborer and I worked up to foreman pipefitter when I retired. I put in twenty-five years in Keyport.—Ben George

Upper left, three-log load. *Lower left, Carrying the Banner*, women protesting low wages. *Upper right*, metal shop at the Cushman Trade School on the Puyallup Indian Reservation. *Lower center*, Port Madison Mills on Bainbridge Island. *Lower right*, Sam Snyder and Louis Napolean at the Port Blakely Mill on Bainbridge Island.

Large photo, Suquamish Indians awaiting a steamer to return them to Bainbridge Island, after attempting to collect their payments for land bought by the government. *Lower, left to right,* real estate advertisements for Chief Seattle Park.

Transition in Labor and Economy

From first contact with western European culture, Puget Sound peoples engaged in a lively system of trade with non-Indians. For a short time during initial settlement the immigrants depended on Indian goods for survival. They acquired dugout canoes for transportation, split cedar board houses for shelter, Indian baskets for food gathering and storage, and dogfish oil to grease the skid roads used for logging. Indians traded these items, as well as salmon and shellfish, in exchange for manufactured goods, which they incorporated into their technology and culture.

As the larger society diversified and became more complex, the occupations of Suquamish people also expanded to meet the needs of the era. Many Indian men and women played a significant role in the local labor force by marketing fish and shellfish and by working in logging camps, sawmills, hopfields, shipyards, and defense industries. The need for monetary income to supplement the increasingly depleted and inaccessible fisheries and forest resources, coupled with changing expectations, caused many Suquamish to seek seasonal employment off the reservation. Nevertheless, most maintained permanent residence within the tribal community.

Hard work and perseverance have long been survival skills of the Suquamish people. For this reason, they were able to make major adjustments to a foreign culture while at the same time continuing their traditional hunting, fishing, and gathering.

Logging. In those days it was dangerous. You could break your back or lose your leg or your arm, something like that ... safety measures. Ain't everybody that's fast enough to get out of the way of a tree when it's falling down.—Bernard Adams

Indians always worked. They worked at the logging camps and worked at the Gamble mill.—William Pickrell

And the clams ... in those days, right after the Depression, if you had a contract with the market, say for three sacks on Monday, three sacks on Wednesday, and maybe four or five on Friday, that meant just what they said. Because there was plenty of people waiting in line to grab that job if you once slipped up. We never had any trouble with the markets.—Bernard Adams

I went to work for the government—I will never forget this date—it was the 29th of May, 1940, and I got into Keyport and I got on a permanent list the same year in November of that year, and I stayed with it. I started right on the bottom as a laborer and I worked up to foreman pipefitter when I retired. I put in twenty-five years in Keyport.—Ben George

Upper left, three-log load. *Lower left, Carrying the Banner*, women protesting low wages. *Upper right*, metal shop at the Cushman Trade School on the Puyallup Indian Reservation. *Lower center*, Port Madison Mills on Bainbridge Island. *Lower right*, Sam Snyder and Louis Napolean at the Port Blakely Mill on Bainbridge Island.

Indians in the Military

The Suquamish Indians have a long history of military service to their tribe and to the United States. In early times Puget Sound tribes established elaborate systems for defending themselves against their enemies. Such was imperative for the protection of the tribe from aggressive neighbors to the north, in British Columbia. Soon after the treaties were negotiated, the Suquamish had their first exposure to modern military training through the boarding schools.

The outbreak of World War I marked a major transition in the history of the Suquamish and other tribes. Indian soldiers willingly joined the armed forces and participated in a conflict in a land they knew little or nothing about. Because of this display of courage and patriotism the Indians were heroes in the hearts of their tribal communities as well as the nation, and were rewarded a long overdue declaration of American citizenship for all Native American peoples by the United States government in 1924.

World War II was readily supported by Suquamish soldiers and citizens through active duty overseas or labor in the war industries at home. The Suquamish Tribe has amongst its members veterans of the two world wars, as well as those in Korea and Vietnam. The tribe remembers with pride those men who perished in battle.

I worked for the ammunition depot, World War II. I worked in the sewing room and I worked in the laundry, I worked in the packing house filling projectiles with powder. I will never forget when I first entered that building, there were 'Danger' signs all over the place and it scared me. 'Danger' here, 'Danger' there! But after you work there awhile you don't pay no attention to it. —Martha George

I went into the Coast Guard. And I was gone for . . . oh, quite a few years. I've been all over the country. I was on the East Coast for seven years. I was from Maine to Florida, Caribbean, Cuba, Panama . . . Mexico . . . Bombay in India, the Mediterranean . . . . Most of this was in World War II. Then I went from there to the South Pacific then, the Philippines . . . I was on a transport, which was transportin' troops when I was in what they call the second battle of the Philippine Sea. I was in eight different battles. One was in North Africa, and Sicily. —James Forsman

Upper left, Tulalip Bulletin *newspaper, June 1918. Lower left, letter from President Truman to Coast Guard veteran James Forsman, 1945. Right, Grace (Sigo) Duggan, John P. Sigo, Bill Sigo, and Eleanor (Sigo) Bagley at Erlands Point, near Chico.*

Sports

Suquamish Ball Team, 1920.

Sports and recreation have always been an important part of Suquamish culture. Traditionally, the native peoples of Puget Sound eagerly competed in various contests such as canoe racing, native weight lifting, jumping, wrestling, running, and swimming. These activities served as tests of strength and courage, as well as opportunities for gaining status and prestige.

Post-contact influences greatly changed the recreational activities in which the Indians participated. These included the introduction of baseball, football, and basketball. Baseball was by far the most popular game, for it required minimal equipment and probably resembled traditional stick games. Well before the turn of the century, Indians of the area demonstrated their fondness of the sport by handcrafting their own bats and in some cases playing barehanded. The Suquamish were famous for their baseball prowess and fielded teams that were well respected throughout Puget Sound. Many Suquamish players managed to earn modest incomes pursuing the sport. By 1920, the Suquamish team had built up such a good reputation due to numerous victories over Indian, as well as non-Indian teams, that they were selected to tour Japan, competing with Asian teams before large audiences.

Today the sporting tradition continues in Suquamish. With the recent completion of the community center gymnasium, basketball has become more popular on the reservation. Tournaments are held annually with tribes throughout the state. The baseball tradition continues with the tribal softball team, which has participated in numerous tournaments, including three on the national level. These activities form a basis for tribal community spirit and identity, while allowing traditional intertribal competition to carry on.

The Indians, through the summer, they'd meet about every week down at the ballground where they formed baseball teams. Seattle had a lot of teams at that time. A lot of them would like to get out of town; they'd come over on the excursion. If they didn't have a team from Seattle, they'd just choose up sides and have a game anyway. That way they finally got acquainted with the non-Indians better because a lot of them liked to play.—Lawrence Webster

I was quite a pretty good amateur baseball player. I played for Suquamish Indians, and I played for Kingston Merchants. I played for Poulsbo a couple a' times, made twenty-four dollars a game sometimes, if I was lucky enough that they picked me to play. About nineteen thirty-two, or three, Port Gamble was startin' a baseball team. And I made the team. And from then on I worked all through the Depression, there, for thirty cents an hour.—Mac Loughrey

Left, Suquamish baseball team. *Right*, Tulalip Indian School girls basketball team.

The Suquamish Tribe Today

Over one hundred years have passed since traditional Suquamish culture began adjusting to white society. While today's culture reflects contemporary society, it still retains close ties with the tribal past. The seven-member governing body, like the earlier chiefs' councils, makes decisions based on the will of all tribal members. Similarly, the Chief Seattle Days Celebration held each August, honoring the memory of the Suquamish chief, re-creates in part the ceremonies of old.

Whereas the Tribal Council and Chief Seattle Days Celebration reflect the Suquamish past, many current tribal programs and enterprises look to the future. Beginning with a Community Health Service Program in 1969, the tribe has since added fisheries and forestry programs, a police department, and planning and business offices. The tribe currently employs fifty people who provide a wide variety of governmental and community services. The tribe will continue to expand employment opportunities for its members, especially in the areas of fisheries and enterprise development.

The Suquamish Museum is housed within the Suquamish Tribal Community Center, which opened April 1980. This building also contains tribal governmental offices and programs, the Tribal Archives, a gymnasium, and kitchen facilities. Indian and non-Indian community residents utilize the building for meetings and recreational purposes.

At the center, plans are developed for land use, fisheries management and enhancement, and social and health services. It is also the site for educational and employment training opportunities. Center activities indeed reflect the vitality of contemporary Suquamish life. By providing continuity with past traditions, tribal programs seek to perpetuate the rich cultural heritage of the Suquamish.

From top to bottom, Suquamish school children, young Chum salmon being transferred from the tribe's Cowling Creek Hatchery, salmon rearing tanks at Grover's Creek. *Center, from top to bottom*, Suquamish Tribal Center, Netarts-style egg incubation raceways, and tribal fisheries lab technician Charlene Ives at Grovers Creek hatchery. *Right*, Merle Hayes planting trees.

Exhibition Artifacts

[Illustrated artifacts are indicated by page numbers in brackets.]

Basket-making materials, cedar bark, limbs and roots, sweet grass and bear grass. [22]

Purse basket, cedar bark, raffia, bear grass, cloth, Suquamish. Amelia Sneatlum, maker. (H: 4 in.; W: 6 in.) Donation, Margaret Adams, 82.1.2.

Clam basket, cedar root, cedar limbs, Suquamish. Martha George, maker, 1980. (H: 11 in.; W: 10 in.) 82.2.1. [22]

Open-weave basket, cedar bark, bear grass, raffia. (H: 4 in.; W: 6½ in.) Donation, Jenny Madell, 82.3.2.

Basket, cedar bark, bear grass, Suquamish. Adeline Alfred Alexis, maker. (H: 9½ in.; W: 12 in.)

Clam basket, cedar limb, cedar bark, Suquamish. Ed Carriere, maker. (H: 11 in.; W: 10 in.) Loan, Ed Carriere, 83.5.6.

Berry picking basket, cedar root, wild cherry bark, bear grass, Suquamish. Louisa Peters, maker. (H: 4½ in.; W: 6½ in.) Loan, Martha George, 83.17.6.

Berry basket, cedar bark and rush, Suquamish. Louisa Peters, maker. Collected by T. T. Waterman, 1919. (H: 6 in.; W: 8 in.) Loan, Burke Museum, 8645.

Coiled basket, salmon gill design. (H: 3 in.; W: 5½ in.) Loan, MOHI, 180.17/139/17.

Child's berry basket, cedar root, bear grass, horsetail root, Suquamish. Celia Jackson, maker. c. 1930. Loan, Trashawndra Henry, 83.8.1.

Berry basket, cedar root, bear grass, Suquamish. Louisa Peters, maker. (H: 10½ in.; W: 14 in.) Loan, Martha George, 83.17.4.

Berry basket, cedar root, bear grass, horsetail root, Suquamish. Celia Jackson, maker, c. 1930. (H: 12 in.; W: 13 in.) Loan, Jim Henry, 83.8.2. [22]

Berry basket, cedar root, wild cherry bark, bear grass, Suquamish. Nancy Ewye, possible maker. (H: 5 in.; W: 8 in.) Loan, Pegie Ahvakana, 83.13.2.

Berry basket, cedar root, wild cherry bark, bear grass, Suquamish. Nancy Ewye, possible maker. (H: 5 in.; W: 6½ in.) Loan, Pegie Ahvakana, 83.13.1.

Berry basket, cedar bark, Suquamish. Louisa Peters, previous owner. (H: 7 in.; W: 8½.) Collected by T. T. Waterman, 1919. Loan, Burke Museum, 8644.

Berry basket, cedar root, bear grass, wild cherry bark, Lucy Riddle (Puyallup), maker. (H: 9½ in.; W: 11 in.) Loan, Oliver Jackson, Sr., 83.7.2. [22]

Berry basket, cedar root, Suquamish. Jacob Wahelchu, maker. c. 1895. (H: 11 in.; W: 16 in.) Loan, Ed Carriere, 83.5.2. [2]

Coiled berry basket, with imbrication. (H: 8½ in.) Loan MOHI, 81.7357.37. [22]

Wooden spoon, probably alder, Skokomish. (L: 10 in.; W: 3½ in.) Loan, Mable Sigo, 83.4.4. [18]

Wooden bowl, probably alder, Skokomish. Nancy Peterson, previous owner. (L: 9 in.; W: 6⅛ in.) Loan, Mable Sigo, 83.4.1. [18]

Bark shredder, whale bone, used for shredding cedar bark. (L: 8 in.; W 5½ in.) Loan, MOHI, 5322.42. [15]

Mat needle, ocean spray wood, used for making cattail mats, Bainbridge Island. (L: 39 in.; W: ½ in.) Loan, Burke Museum, T-20.

Mat needle, ocean spray wood (ironwood) used in making cattail mats, Suquamish. Jacob Wahelchu, maker. (L: 38 in.; W: ½ in.) Loan, Ed Carriere, 83.5.5. [25]

Mat creaser, wood, Suquamish. Annie Rodgers, previous owner. (H: 2¾ in.; W: 6 in.) Collected by T. T. Waterman, 1919. Loan, Burke Museum, 8624. [25]

Mat fragment, cattail, cedar bark. Loan, Martha George, 83.17.10. [24]

Coiled basket, salmon gill design. (H: 8½ in.; W: 10 in.) Loan, MOHI 888.1.

Salish weaving loom, cedar, replica. Robin K. Wright, maker, 1983. (H: 57 in.; W: 46½ in.) [27]

Salish blanket, wool, Lummi. Fran and Bill James, makers. (L: 100 in.; W: 40 in.) Loan, Barbara Lawrence and Bryan Alldredge. [24]

Spindle whorl and stick, cedar replica. Robin K. Wright, maker, 1983. (L: 35 in.; W: 5 in.)

Cedar mat, cedar bark, bear grass, cherry bark, replica of Makah mat, Suquamish. Ed Carriere, maker, 1982. (L: 43 in.; W: 27½ in.) Loan, Ed Carriere, 83.5.4. [24]

Mat, cedar bark, purchased from Indian woman selling items at Winslow, 1906. (L: 60½ in.; W: 37½ in.) Loan, Ella Wallace Selland, Bainbridge Island Historical Society, 83.18.1. [25]

Mat, cattail, cedar bark. Loan, Burke Museum. [25]

Grease bowl, alder replica. Robin K. Wright, maker, 1983. (H: 4½ in.; W: 6½ in.)

Bark shredder, maple replica. Robin K. Wright, maker, 1983. (L: 14 in.; W: 5 in.)

Rattle, cedar, Salish. Gene Jones, Sr., maker, 1984. (L: 11 in.; W: 3½ in.) Loan by artist.

Mat creaser, Salish. Gene Jones, Sr., maker, 1984. (H: 4½ in.; L: 9 in.) Loan by artist.

Two "cobble choppers," prehistoric stone cutting tools found locally, indicating long occupation in this area. (H: 4 in.; W: 4 in.) 83.30.1-2.

Lithic point. (L: 2½ in.; W: 2 in.) Loan, Burke Museum, B346.

Point, stone. (L: 2½ in.; W: 1½ in.) Loan, Burke Museum, B372.

Lithic Point, stone. (L: 2½ in.; W: ¾ in.) Loan, Burke Museum, B122414.

Stone maul, northwest coast, probably Tlingit. (H: 7½ in.; W: 4½ in.) Loan, Burke Museum, 1-381. [18]

Adze handle, wood, Klallam. (L: 8½ in.; W: 1½ in.) Loan, Gene Jones, Sr., 82.5. [29]

Adze blade, stone, Suquamish. (L: 6½ in.; W: 1½ in.) Donation, Bernard Adams, 82.5.1. [29]

Hand adze, used in making racing canoes, wood, iron blade, Suquamish. Jack Adams, maker. (L: 7½ in.; W: 3½ in.) Loan, MOHI, 5072.68. [29]

Duck float. Cedar replica, Skokomish type. Robin K. Wright, maker, 1983. (H: 8½ in.; L: 16 in.; W: 6½ in.) [21]

Beaver pelt. (L: 29 in.; W: 27 in.) Loan, Leota Anthony.

Seal pelt. (L: 33½ in.; W: 22½ in.) Loan, Charles Sigo.

Clam basket, cedar root, cedar limbs, Suquamish. Bernard Adams, maker. (H: 12 in.; W: 15 in.) Loan, MOHI.

Fish hook, Salish type, replica. Robin K. Wright, maker, 1983. (L: 3 in.; W: 1 in.) [20]

Berry picker, ocean spray wood and string, Suquamish, pre-1928. (L: 22¾ in.; W: 2½ in.) From H.E. Holmes estate. Loan, Burke Museum, 1-10515. [19]

Toggling spear point, for seal hunting. (L: 5 in.; w: 1 in.) Loan, MOHI, 1241. [21]

Salmon club, wood, Skokomish. Dick Lewis, maker. (L: 18½ in.; W: 2 in.) Washington World's Fair Commission, previous owner. Loan, Burke Museum, 60. [19]

Spoon, cow horn, Suquamish. (L: 8½ in.; W: 2⅝ in.) Loan, Lillian Jones, 83.12.1. [18]

Wooden spoon, probably alder, Suquamish. (L: 9½ in.; W: 3¼ in.) Annie Rodgers, previous owner. Collected by T. T. Waterman, 1919. Loan, Burke Museum, 8615. [18]

Wooden spoon, alder, Suquamish. (L: 10½ in.; W: 3½ in.) Mary Sam, previous owner. Collected by T. T. Waterman, 1919. Loan, Burke Museum, 8618. [18]

Wooden bowl, probably alder, Skokomish. (L: 14½ in.; W: 10¾ in.) Loan, Mable Sigo, 83.4.2. [18]

Berry basket, cedar root, bear grass, Suquamish. Celia Jackson, maker, c. 1930. (H: 13 in.; w: 15 in.) Loan, Oliver Jackson, Sr., 83.7.1.

Dugout war canoe, cedar, Quileute. (L: 18 ft.; W: 42 in.) Loan, Kitsap County Historical Society.

Dugout hunting canoe, made in Port Madison area. This thin hulled, finely made canoe has been much altered over the years, including the removal of the stern and prow pieces. (L: 16 ft.; W: 31 in.) Loan, Bob Riebe.

Herring rake, wood with iron nails, Bainbridge Island. (L: 113 in.; W: 4 in.) Collected by Mrs. Walter Waters, 1920s. Loan, Burke Museum, 1-1670. [21]

Woman's canoe paddle, maple with ochre paint. George Kliwha, maker. (L: 50 in.; W: 5¾ in.) Louisa Peters, previous owner. Collected by T.T. Waterman, 1919. Loan, Burke Museum, 8633. [28]

Anchor stone, Suquamish. (H: 12 in.; W: 9½ in.) Loan, Bob George, Sr., 83.17.1. [28]

Anchor, stone, Suquamish. (H: 7 in.; W: 8 in.) Loan, Craig P. Campbell, 83.11.1.

Fish weir segment, wood branches, roots, Tacoma. (H: 46 in.; W: 21 in.) Loan, Burke Museum, 1983-35/11.

Twined basket, cedar root, bear grass, cherry bark, Suquamish. (H: 6 in.; W: 9½ in.) Collected by Mr. and Mrs. Arthur Wilcox. Loan, Burke Museum, 2.5E545.

Twined basket, wolf design, Skokomish. (H: 4½ in.; W: 6½ in.) Loan, MOHI, 2735.1. [23]

Pestle, stone, Puget Sound. (H: 6½ in.; W: 4 in.) Loan, Dorothy Case Nystrom, 83.19.1.

Salmon roasting tong, Madrona, Suquamish. (L: 37 in.; W: 1½ in.) Louisa Peters, previous owner. Collected by T. T. Waterman, 1919. Loan, Burke Museum, 8631.

Clam digging stick, Madrona. Suquamish. (L: 29 in.; W 1 in.) Mary Adams, previous owner. Collected by T. T. Waterman, 1919. Loan, Burke Museum, 8632.

Cooking sticks, wood, Suquamish. (L: 33 in.; W 1 in.) Louisa Peters, previous owner. Collected by T. T. Waterman, 1919. Loan, Burke Museum, #8630c-f.

Berry basket, cedar root, bear grass, wild cherry. (H: 9 in.; W: 8½ in.) Loan, Pegie Ahvakana, 83.13.3.

Coiled basket, with imbrication. (H: 10 in.; W: 13 in.) Loan, MOHI, 190/g.

Halibut hook. (L: 10 in.; W: 2 in.) Loan, MOHI, 1475.2. [20]

Blanket pin, bone. (L: 3½ in.; W: ¼ in.) Loan, MOHI, 4980.6. [24]

Mat needle, bone. (L: 6 in.; W: ¼ in.) Loan, MOHI, 4673.60. [24]

Coiled basket, cedar root, bear grass, wild cherry bark. (H: 6½ in.; W: 9 in.) Donation, Jenny Madell, 82.3.4.

Berry picking basket, cedar root, wild cherry bark, bear grass, Suquamish. Mary Wesiduck Jacob, maker, c. 1895. (H: 10 in.; W: 14 in.) Loan, Ed Carriere, 83.5.

Berry basket with tumpline, cedar root, bear grass, wild cherry bark. Suquamish. Lucy Kuker, maker. (H: 9½ in.; W: 13 in.) Loan, Martha George, 83.17.2.

Berry basket, cedar root, wild cherry bark, Suquamish. Louisa Peters, previous owner and possible maker. (H: 10½ in.; W: 13½ in.) Loan, Martha George, 83.17.5.

Basket dolls, sweetgrass, raffia, Suquamish. Gloria Smith, maker, 1983. (H: 5 in.; W: 3 in.) 83.41.1-2. [22]

Ceremonial headband, shredded cedar bark, Suquamish. (Diam. 12 in.; H: 1½ in.) Jack Davis, previous owner. Collected by T.T. Waterman, 1919. Loan, Burke Museum, 8640. [30]

Bead necklace, glass seed beads, thread, Suquamish, pre-1928. (Diam.: 6½ in.) Annie Rodgers, previous owner. From H. E. Holmes estate. Loan, Burke Museum, 1-10531.

Bead necklace, glass bead and mountain sheep horn pendant, Suquamish. (Diam.: 4 in.) Annie Rodgers, previous owner. From H. E. Holmes estate, pre-1928. Loan, Burke Museum, 1-10526.

Deer hoof rattle, with buckskin, Suquamish. (L: 7 in.; W: 1½ in.) Jack Davis, previous owner (belonged to grandmother). Collected by T. T. Waterman, 1919. Loan, Burke Museum, 8638. [30]

Necklace, tradebeads, shellbeads, brass token, dentalium. (Diam.: 8 in.) Donation, Meta Heller, 83.16.1.

Hand drum, wood, hide, string, and copper nails, Suquamish, pre-1928. (Diam.: 20 in.; H: 2¼ in.) From H. E. Holmes estate. Loan, Burke Museum, 10534b. [31]

Drum stick, wood, red wool fabric, and string, Suquamish, pre-1928. (L: 12 in.; W: 2 in.) From H.E. Holmes estate. Loan, Burke Museum, 1-10534a. [31]

Necklace, dentalia, trade beads, coins. (L: 34 in.; W: 7 in.) Loan, MOHI. [32]

Mask, cedar, Suquamish. (H: 13 in.; W: 8 in.; D: 5 in.) Sam Snyder, previous owner. Loan, Burke Museum, 2.5E1002. [31]

Bird rattle, wood, Bainbridge Island. (L: 14 in.; W: 3¼ in.) Collected by Ralph Altman, 1920s. Loan, Burke Museum, 1-1848. [31]

Duck rattle, wood. (L: 17 in.; W: 4 in.) Loan, MOHI, 1694/1.

Salish whistle, cedar, twine. Gene Jones, Sr., maker, 1983. (L: 8½ in.; W: 1½ in.)

Ceremonial staff, cedar. Gene Jones, Sr., maker, 1983. (L: 55 in.; W: 2½ in.) Loan by artist.

Hide dressing tool, bone, Suquamish. Probably made by Jack Adams. (L: 8 in.; W: 2 in.) Mary Adams, previous owner. Collected by T. T. Waterman, 1919. Loan, Burke Museum, 8622.

Twined basket, mountain goat design, Skokomish. (H: 3 in.; W: 4 in.) Loan, MOHI, 3334.13.

Saltwater canoe model. (L: 31 in.; W: 5 in.) Loan, MOHI, 7084.1.

Clam basket, cedar root, Suquamish. Celia Jackson, maker. c. 1975. (H: 12 in.; W: 14 in.) Loan, Oliver Jackson, Sr., 83.7.3.

Canoe bailer, cedarbark. (H: 5 in.; W: 7 in.) Loan, MOHI. [28]

Clam digging sticks, Suquamish. William Sigo, Sr., maker, c. 1975. (L: 23 in.; W: 1 in.) Loan, Mable Sigo, 83.4.5-7. [19]

One-man hunting canoe, cedar, Suquamish. Louisa Peters, previous owner. (L: 13 ft.; W: 23½ in.) Collected by T. T. Waterman, 1919. Loan, Burke Museum, 8670.

Canoe paddle, probably maple, Suquamish. Charlie Winayule, possible maker. (L: 39 in.; W: 5½ in.) Loan, Chuck Deam, 82.2.1. [28]

Canoe paddle, probably maple, Suquamish. (L: 57 in.; W: 6 in.) Annie and William Rodgers, previous owners. Donation, Holmes Operating Company, 83.1.1.

Canoe bow piece, cedar, Tulalip, pre-1927. (L: 58 in.; W: 20 in.) Loan, Burke Museum, 1-10548. [28]

Chief Seattle Day program, 1912. Loan, John Crowell.

Chief Seattle Days—1912 coin. (Diam.: 1½ in.) Loan, Chuck Deam, 83.15.1.

Chief Seattle Days buttons. Loans, Pegie Ahvakana, Bev Mott, Bernard Adams. [37]

Slahal bones, used in bone game, Suquamish. (L: 3 in.; W: 1½ in.) Sam Snyder, previous owner. Donation, Margaret Adams, 82.1.1 a-d. [33]

Gambling discs, wood, cedar bark, Snohomish. (Diam.: 2 in.) Mrs. Agnes James, previous owner. Loan, Burke, 1-137. [33]

Misc. logging tools. Loans, MOHI, Kitsap County Historical Society, Toby James, Mac Loughrey, James Forsman, and Gene Jones, Sr.

"Fall" gill net, nylon, polyethylene corks, twine, used in fall for coho and chum salmon, 1980. Donation, Suquamish Tribal Fisheries, 83.14.1.

"Chinook" salmon gill net, cedar floats. Loan, Merle Hayes.

Army cap. Loan, MOHI, M-580.

Army cap. Loan, MOHI, M-725.

World War I army hat. Loan, MOHI, M-691.

World War I helmet. Loan, MOHI, M-760.

Tulalip Bulletin Newspaper, original, June 1918. Loan, Burke Museum.

Letter, recognition from White House to veterans, 1945. Loan, James Forsman, 83.24.12.

Misc. personal military medals, pins, bars, etc. Loan, James Forsman.

Catalogue Photographs

Page 2	Little Joe and wife (Snohomish) next to a large dugout canoe on the Tulalip Indian Reservaion. STA 0847.
Page 13	*Suquamish Woman*, by E. S. Curtis, 1899. STA 1105.
Page 13	*Voyage of Discovery*, an account of Captain George Vancouver's exploration. Title page and excerpt from journal. STA 1894.
Page 14	Northern Puget Sound longhouse, possibly at Tulalip or La Conner, 1913. STA 1323.
Page 14–15	Group at Old Man House Village on Agate Pass, c. 1875. The long beam is the last remnant of the 500-foot-long structure known as Old Man House. STA 1770.
Page 15	Chief Kitsap's family, from early tintype photograph, c.1850-60. STA 1647.
Page 15	Young Muckleshoot girl in traditional cedar bark clothing, c. 1910. STA 0901.
Page 16	Salish summer camping site, c. 1900. STA 1372.
Page 16–17	Suquamish village at Eagle Harbor on Bainbridge Island, c. 1905. STA 0839.
Page 18–19	William We-ah-lup (Tulalip) drying salmon and salmon eggs in the traditional manner, 1906. STA 1075.
Page 20	Fishing for Chinook salmon with gill net. STA 1333.
Page 21	An Indian couple drying fish on racks. STA 0850.
Page 23	Tennessee, a Suquamish basket maker, at her home at Port Blakely on Bainbridge Island, c. 1910. STA 0054.
Page 23	Basket maker. STA 1895.
Page 24	*The Tule Gatherer*, by E. S. Curtis, 1910. STA 1136.
Page 25	*Fishing Camp—Skokomish*, by E. S. Curtis, 1912. STA 1133.
Page 28–29	Camp on Ballast Island, in Seattle, near traditional camping site taken over by city expansion, c. 1880. STA 1896.
Page 29	Jennie Davis and Annie Rodgers in a cedar dugout canoe, by H.E. Holmes, c. 1910. STA 0155.
Page 30	Companion and Annie Rodgers. Note ceremonial staff, duck rattle, cedar bark and feather headdress, and mussel shell necklace held and worn by Annie Rogers. STA 1357.
Page 31	Group at blessing of Chief Sealth's grave, during Chief Seattle Days, 1920. Visible in photograph: Joe George, Annie Rodgers, Stephanie Kitsap, Louisa Peters, Sam Wilson, Tom Ewye, George Ewye. STA 0006.
Page 32	Group of Indians at Chief Seattle Days, 1912. Jack Davis *(sitting in front)*, Ellen Rodgers, Louisa Peters, Jennie Davis, Annie Rodgers, Stephanie Kitsap, two unidentified, Suzie Napoleon *(first row, left to right)*, Mary Adams, William Rodgers, George Ewye *(second row)*, Joe George and Sam Snyder in back row with hats. STA 1358.
Page 32	Skokomish woman in wool garment with ceremonial objects, 1886. Note necklace similar to artifact in this book. STA 1908.
Page 33	Suquamish Indians working in the hop fields, c. 1890. STA 345.
Page 33	Trolling for salmon in saltwater canoe, 1897. STA 0843.
Page 33	Indian group gambling on beach near Tacoma, c. 1885. STA 1893.
Page 35	Treaty Protest, Olympia, c. 1864. A group of Suquamish leaders at Olympia in 1864, protesting that the government had not yet established a reservation for the tribe as promised in the Treaty of Point Elliott nine years earlier. Among those pictured are important Suquamish leaders: William Kitsap, Jim Seattle, Big John, Jacob Wahelchu, William Chico and Steve Wilson. STA 0104.
Page 35	*Point Elliott Treaty*, excerpts, 1855. STA 1897.
Page 36	Jim Seattle, son of Chief Seattle, 1867. STA 0104.
Page 36	Angeline, daughter of Chief Seattle. STA 1898.
Page 36	*Chief Seattle* (Sealth and Seattle are both anglicized versions of the Chief's Salish name.), by E. M. Sammis, 1865. STA 1646.
Page 37	Welcoming dance at Chief Seattle Days, 1912. STA 1091.
Page 37	Procession dance at Chief Seattle Days, 1912. *(Right to left)* Peter Rodgers (with drum), William Rodgers, Jack Davis, Joe George, George Ewye, Sam Snyder, Annie Rodgers. STA 0162.
Page 38	St. George's Mission School on the Puyallup Indian Reservation, c. 1890. STA 1390.
Page 39	Father F. Chirouse and his Indian students at Tulalip, 1865. One of the earliest known photographs of Puget Sound Indians. STA 1088.
Page 40	Lena and Clara Siddle, Tulalip Indian School, 1912. STA 1521.
Page 41	Line-up of boys, Cushman Trade School, 1908 or 1909. Lawrence Webster, former Tribal Chairman, near the far left in back row. STA 1419.
Page 41	House boys, 1908. Lawrence Webster is fifth from left. STA 1422.
Page 41	Kitchen girls, Tulalip Indian School, c. 1908. STA 1434.
Page 41	Cushman Trade School Band, Point Defiance Park, Tacoma, 1914. STA 0449.
Page 42–43	A group of Suquamish Indians on Seattle's Colman Dock, c. 1906. The group was awaiting a steamer to return them to Eagle Harbor, Bainbridge Island, after attempting to collect their payments for land bought by the government at the original site of Old Man House Village and the surrounding area. STA 0837.
Page 42–43	Real estate advertisement—Chief Seattle Park, c. 1952. STA 1899.
Page 44	Three-log load, Port Gamble, 1923. Lawrence Webster, middle. STA 0534.
Page 44	*Carrying The Banner:* women protesting low wages. STA 0496.
Page 45	Metal shop at the Cushman Trade School on the Puyallup Indian Reservation, c. 1914. STA 1388.
Page 45	Port Madison Mills, by LaRoche. Bainbridge Island, c. 1900. The spit in the background is the site of an early Suquamish village. STA 1687.
Page 45	Sam Snyder and Louis Napoleon after they had worked at the Port Blakely Mill on Bainbridge Island. STA 1716.
Page 46	*Tulalip Bulletin* newspaper, June 1918. STA 1900.
Page 46	Letter from President Truman to Coast Guard veteran James Forsman, 1945. STA 1907.
Page 47	*Left to right*, Grace Sigo Duggan, John P. Sigo, Bill Sigo, Jr., Eleanor (Sigo) Bagley at Erlands Point, near Chico, 1942. STA 0412.
Page 48	Suquamish baseball team, 1920, by Cowan. *(Left to right, front)* Ed Pratt, Jimmy Smith, Harold Belmont; *(back)* Tom Henry, David Dan, Edward Alfred, Woody Loughrey, William Kitsap, Tom Philips, and Charley Thompson. STA 1843.
Page 49	Tulalip Indian School girls' basketball team, 1910. STA 1625.
Page 50	Suquamish school children, 1983. STA 1903.
Page 50	Young Chum salmon being transferred from Cowlings Creek hatchery, 1983. STA 1905.
Page 50	Salmon rearing tanks inside the tribe's Grover's Creek Hatchery: technician Charlene Ives, 1983. STA 1906.
Page 51	Netarts-style egg incubation raceways, at Cowlings Creek Hatchery. This facility has a rearing capacity of 1.5 million Chum salmon. The tribe's broodstock source is native East Kitsap Chum salmon, 1983. STA 1904.
Page 51	Tribal fisheries technician Charlene Ives at Grovers Creek Hatchery, 1983. STA 1902.
Page 51	Merle Hayes planting trees, part of the tribal forestry program, 1983. STA 1901.

Bibliography

Amoss, P. *Coast Salish Spirit Dancing*. Seattle: University of Washington Press, 1978.

Curtis, E. *The North American Indian*. Volume IX. Morwood, MA: The Plimpton Press, 1915.

Gustafson, P. *Salish Weaving*. Seattle: University of Washington Press, 1980.

Haeberlin, H., and E. Gunther. *Indians of Puget Sound*. Seattle: University of Washington Press, 1930.

Heuving, J. *Suquamish Today*. Seattle: United Indians of All Tribes Foundation, 1979.

Holm, B. *Box of Daylight, Northwest Coast Indian Art*. Seattle: Seattle Art Museum, 1983.

Kew, J. *Sculpture and Engraving of the Central Coast Salish Indians*. Vancouver: U.B.C. Museum of Anthropology, 1980.

Lane, B. *Identity, Treaty Status, and Fisheries of the Suquamish Tribe of the Port Madison Reservation*. Washington, D.C.: Report for U.S. Department of the Interior, 1974.

Ruby, R., and J. Brown. *Myron Eells and the Puget Sound Indians*. Seattle: Superior Publishing Company, 1976.

Smith, M. *Puyallup-Nisqually*. New York: Columbia University Press, 1940.

Snyder, W. *Southern Puget Sound Salish: Texts, Place Names, and Dictionary*. Sacramento: Sacramento Anthropological Society, 1968.

Stewart, H. *Indian Artifacts of the Northwest Coast*. Seattle: University of Washington Press, 1973.

Stewart, H. *Indian Fishing: Early Methods on the Northwest Coast*. Seattle: University of Washington Press, 1977.

Stewart, H. *Cedar*. Seattle: University of Washington Press, 1984.

Thompson, N., and C. Marr. *Crow's Shells: Artistic Basketry of Puget Sound*. Seattle: Dushuyay Publications, 1983.

Underhill, R. *Indians of the Pacific Northwest*. Riverside, CA: U.S. Office of Indian Affairs, Education Division, Sherman Institute Press, 1945.

Waterman, T.T. *Notes on the Ethnology of the Indians of Puget Sound*. New York: Museum of the American Indian/Heye Foundation, 1973.

Waterman, T.T. and R. Griener. *Indian Houses of Puget Sound*. New York: Indian Notes and Monographs, Misc. Series IX.

Wingert, P. *American Indian Sculpture*. New York: Hacker Art Books, 1949.